GUITAR

ON TAP!

WISE PUBLICATIONS
London / New York / Sydney / Paris / Copenhagen / Madrid / Tokyo

Exclusive distributors:
Music Sales Limited
8/9 Frith Street, London W1V 5TZ, England.
Music Sales Pty Limited
120 Rothschild Avenue, Rosebery, NSW 2018, Australia.

Order No.AM962214
ISBN 0-7119-7996-0
This book © Copyright 2000 by Wise Publications.

Written by Joe Bennett.
Book design & layout by Digital Music Art
Cover design by Michael Bell Design
Text Photographs by George Taylor
Artist photographs courtesy of LFI.

Printed in the United Kingdom by
Caligraving Limited, Thetford, Norfolk.

Your Guarantee of Quality:
As publishers, we strive to produce every book to the highest commercial standards.
The music has been freshly engraved and the book has been carefully
designed to minimise awkward page turns and to make playing from it a real pleasure.
Particular care has been given to specifying acid-free,
neutral-sized paper made from pulps which have not been elemental chlorine bleached.
This pulp is from farmed sustainable forests and was produced with special regard for the environment.
Throughout, the printing and binding have been planned to ensure
a sturdy, attractive publication which should give years of enjoyment.
If your copy fails to meet our high standards, please inform us and we will gladly replace it.

Music Sales' complete catalogue describes thousands of titles and
is available in full colour sections by subject, direct from Music Sales Limited.
Please state your areas of interest and send a cheque/postal order for £1.50 for postage to:
Music Sales Limited, Newmarket Road, Bury St. Edmunds, Suffolk IP33 3YB.

www.musicsales.com

Guitar Chords To Go!

How often have you looked in a chord book and seen a load of shapes you don't understand? Or even worse, played the chord line from a songbook only to find that the guitar part sounds nothing like the original recording?

Guitarists can learn in two different ways – study or trial and error. The only trouble is, sometimes the chords you study aren't the same as the ones you actually use when you're playing. The purpose of this book is to guide you through the chord shapes which guitarists use most of the time. It's not intended to cover every chord that was ever invented – there's no chapter on jazz, for example – but it does contain the shapes that the majority of working guitarists use when they're playing live or recording. We've even included 'lazy' shapes which, technically speaking, constitute 'bad' technique. But if everyone else is using these chords and creating great music with them, why should you miss out?

Diagrams explained

Fretboxes

Fretboxes show the guitar upright *i.e.* with the headstock, nut and tuning pegs at the top of the picture – six vertical lines represent the strings.

The x symbol means you should not play this string

The o symbol means play the string 'open' without fretting a note

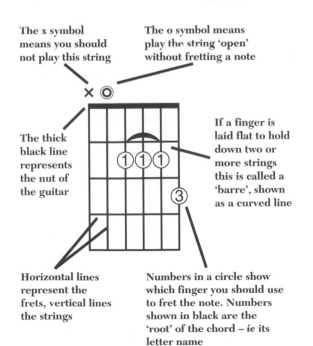

The thick black line represents the nut of the guitar

If a finger is laid flat to hold down two or more strings this is called a 'barre', shown as a curved line

Horizontal lines represent the frets, vertical lines the strings

Numbers in a circle show which finger you should use to fret the note. Numbers shown in black are the 'root' of the chord – ie its letter name

Notation and tablature

'Tab' is drawn with the guitar on its side, with the thickest string at the bottom – six horizontal lines represent the strings.

The top stave shows the chord as it would appear in traditional music notation

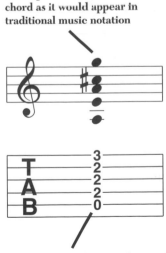

Below is the tablature – the numbers represent the fret positions. A zero means the string should be played open

Open major chords

One of the simplest and most common types of chord is the 'major'. They have a very simple, uncomplicated sound, and as such are often used in folk and country music. The major chords in this section are played in an 'open' position, meaning that one or more of the strings you strum is not fretted. Open chords are, most of the time, the easiest type to play.

You can hear major chords in almost every type of music. These examples have all been used at one time or another by artists as diverse as Buddy Holly, The Beatles, Bob Dylan, Oasis, The Eagles, Queen and The Verve. In gig set lists and chord sheets, they're generally referred to by their letter name only, so the word 'major' is omitted – *e.g.* C major is usually just referred to as C.

A

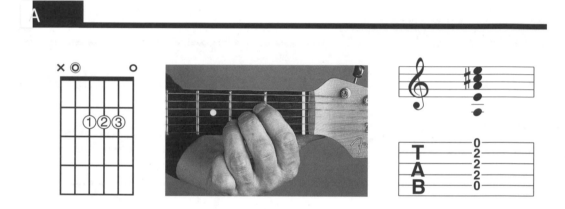

Don't strum the sixth (thickest) string. You may find it tricky to squeeze three fingers together in a row like this – some rock players cover all three notes by squeezing the second and third fingers together.

C

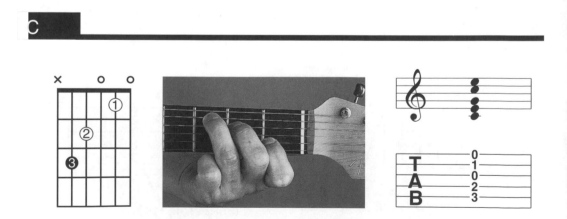

C is more difficult because one of the open strings comes between the fretted notes.

Keep all your fingers at right angles to the fingerboard to let the open strings ring freely.

C (version 2)

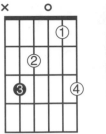

This version of the open C chord has a slightly fuller sound due to the top G note which is added by the little finger. It's often used by folk-rock acoustic players like Bob Dylan and Paul Simon.

D

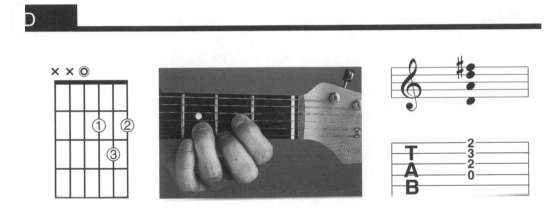

Most players think of D as a triangle shape on the neck. Avoid strumming the sixth and fifth strings.

E

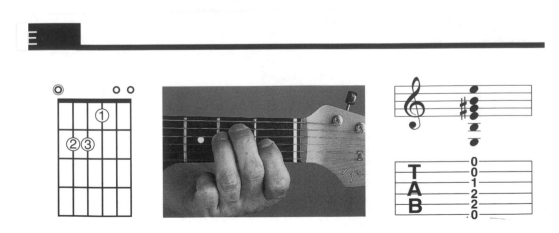

The chord beloved of Marc Bolan, John Lennon and Noel Gallagher. E has a rich, full sound, because it contains three open notes, and you can strum all six strings.

F

Although not strictly an open chord (*i.e.* it doesn't contain open strings) this easy F is shown here because of its 1st fret position. Note that the first finger is flattened across two strings in a 'barre'.

G

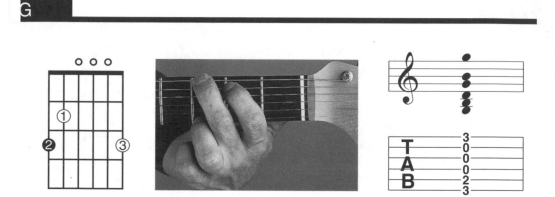

G is another full-sounding chord, but it can take work to master that nasty stretch between the second and third fingers. Make sure that you're not accidentally muting any of the open strings.

G (version 2)

Some guitarists play a G chord with four fingers, as shown here. It gives more of a rock feel, and you'll see it under the fingers of Tom Petty and Bruce Springsteen, among others.

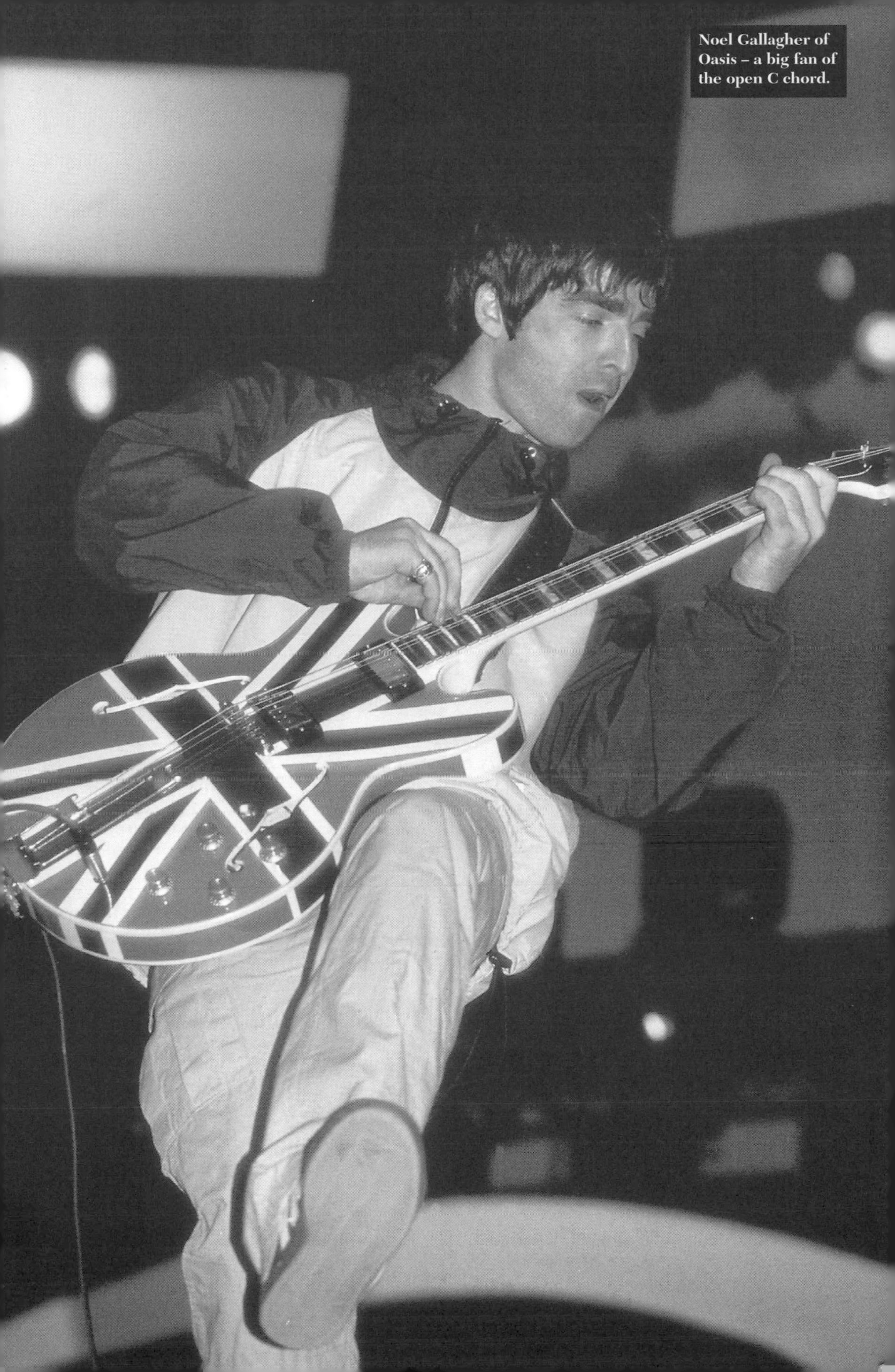

Noel Gallagher of Oasis – a big fan of the open C chord.

Open minor chords

If every songwriter only ever played major chords, the world would never have heard Paul Weller's *Wild Wood*, John Lennon's *Working Class Hero* or Metallica's *Nothing Else Matters*. Minor chords have a melan-choly edge which some musicians describe as 'sad-sounding', although this isn't always the case – check out the up-tempo verse of *I Wanna Be Like You* from the movie *The Jungle Book*, or the intro from the blues classic *Hit The Road Jack*.

The three minor chords shown here have been used in thousands of songs, and are among the first chords every guitar player needs to learn. Usually, they are combined with other types of chords (such as majors, 7ths, minor 7ths etc) – it's rare for a piece of music to feature minor chords alone.

Am

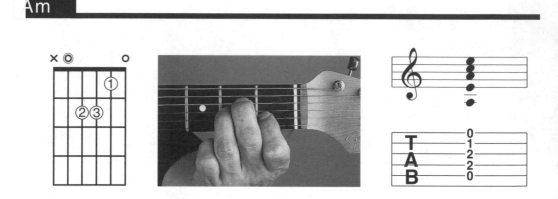

This is the first chord in The Animals' *House Of The Rising Sun* and The Rolling Stones' *Angie*, among many others. Make sure you don't catch the sixth string accidentally – this will make it sound muddy.

Dm

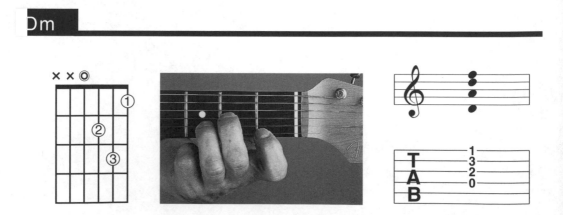

Although D minor is only a four-string chord (so don't strum the two bass strings) it has a slightly sweeter sound than A minor. Practise it until all four strings sound clearly.

Em

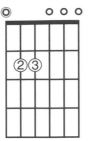

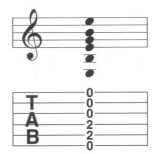

This dramatic-sounding chord is the easiest of the three minor shapes. As long as you make sure that both fingers are cleanly and accurately fretting the notes, E minor will always sound great.

John Lennon used open Am as the first chord of his song *Working Class Hero.*

Open seventh chords

Seventh chords sound more complicated and colourful than their major and minor cousins. They come in three basic types – 'ordinary' 7ths (sometimes called dominant 7ths), major 7ths, and minor 7ths. You may notice that some of the major 7ths shapes are similar to their corresponding major chord, and some of the minor 7ths are similar to their corresponding minor chord.

For this reason, 7th-type chords are often used in place of more straightforward majors and minors.

Ordinary 7ths sometimes appear in blues, rock and R&B. Major 7ths have a wistful quality and consequently sound good in ballads. Minor 7ths can add a jazzy or funky sound to your chord sequence. Note the way they are abbreviated – 7, maj7 and m7.

A7

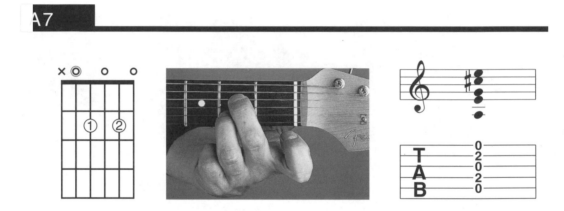

This is basically an ordinary A chord with one finger taken off, though feel free to use different fingers from the ones shown here if you find it easier to make the notes sound clearly.

A7 (version 2)

Although it's less common than the basic shape, many players still prefer this version of A7. It's tricky though, because you have to barre across three strings with the first finger.

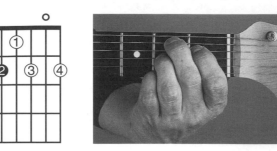

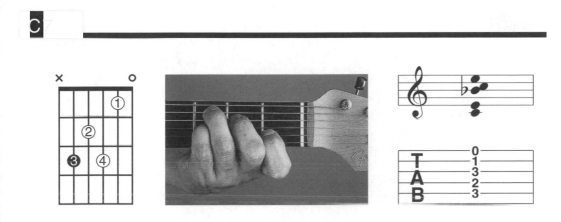

Yes, it's awkward, but the chord of B7 is essential to learn, not least because it appears in the most common guitar-based chord sequence in the world – the 12-bar blues in E.

If you add your little finger to a normal C major chord you get this open version of C7. Hint – move this shape up two frets and play only the middle four strings for a different D7 (see page 38).

This is the more common version of D7 though, as used by folkies the world over. It sounds very 'country' if you play it before or after a G chord, or more bluesy when it occurs after an A7 chord.

E7

If you're ever going to play the blues, you need this chord. It's another example of a major chord

(E major) with a finger removed, creating a 7th. Make sure the open fourth string rings clearly.

F#7

Although you don't see this chord as often as some of the others in this chapter, it's a useful open

chord in its own right – note that it's quite similar to the F shape on page 6.

G7

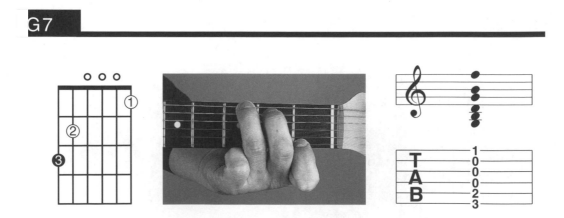

The open chord of G7 looks similar to an ordinary G major (page 6), but check out that fingering –

you'll find that you have to move all three fingers to change between the chords of G and G7.

Am7

Take a finger off an A minor chord and you get
open Am7. Note that the sixth string is not played.

Dm7

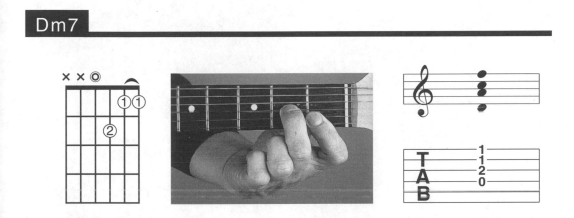

This chord can be played with the first finger
flattened over two strings, as shown here, or by
using three separate fingers for the three fretted
notes. This is the version most people find easiest.

Em7

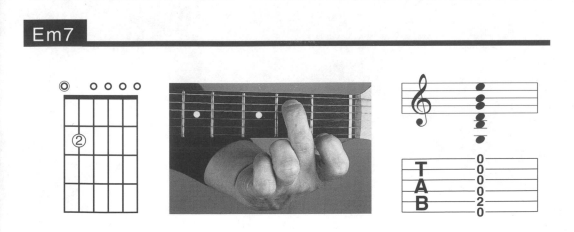

One finger and five open strings – what could be
simpler than that?!

Paul Simon used the dreamy sound of major 7th chords in the songs of Simon & Garfunkel.

Amaj7

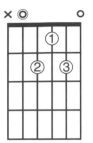

Although the fingering of this chord appears to be similar to the open D7 (page 11), it sounds very different. Try playing a chord of A, followed by Amaj7, followed by A7 for a classic Beatles effect.

Cmaj7

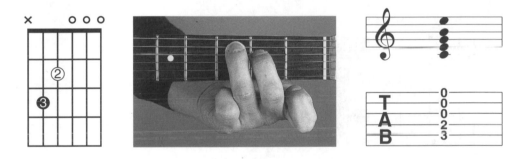

Play a C chord, then remove the first finger, letting the open second string sound as shown.

Dmaj7

Dmaj7 can be played either of two ways – with three separate fingers, as shown here, or with one finger flattened across the first three strings. Make sure the open fourth string rings clearly.

17

Emaj7

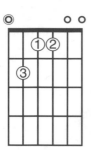  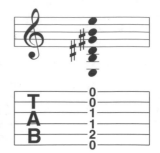

This open maj7 shape is not used by many players because it sometimes jars slightly on the ear, but there are times (especially in country strumming or single-note picked chord parts) when it works fine.

Fmaj7

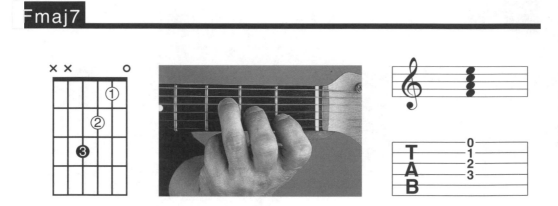

This 'diagonal' shape sounds lovely when it's played before or after a C or Cmaj7 chord.

Gmaj7

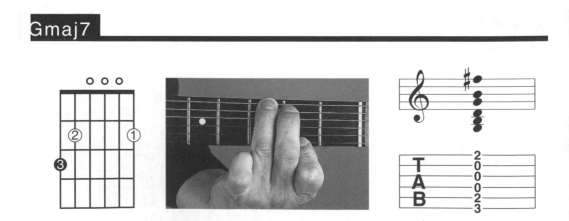

This is the big, expansive chord that is played in the verse of The Eagles' track *Lyin' Eyes*.

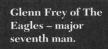
Glenn Frey of The Eagles – major seventh man.

4

Barre chords

Barre chords are so-called because one of the fretting hand's fingers is pressed against two or more strings (this is shown as a curved line in the fretbox). They can be moved up or down the neck to different fret positions to create new chords. The advantage of this is that once you've learned one new barre shape, you've in effect learned 12 new chords!

Below are diagrams showing the names of the notes on the sixth and fifth strings. To find any barre chord, look at the fretbox to see whether the root note (shown in a black circle) appears on the fifth or sixth string, then move the barre shape up or down until you reach the desired pitch. For example, a chord of A♭ (also known as G♯) can be played using an 'F shape' moved up to the 4th fret.

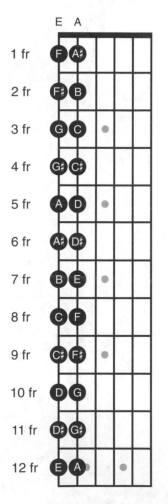

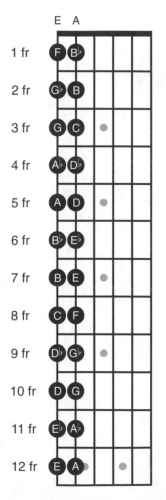

This diagram shows how to find any barre chord position, and will help you if the chord you want has a sharp (♯) in its name. All of the F-based barre shapes in this book (see opposite) have their root on the sixth string – the B♭-based ones have theirs on the fifth.

Use this version if the chord you want has a flat (♭) in its name. Both of these diagrams can be used to find any barre chord which has its root on the sixth or fifth string – simply select the type you want (minor, maj7, 7 etc) then find the letter name (F, G, D♭ etc) on the fingerboard.

F

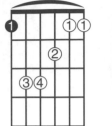  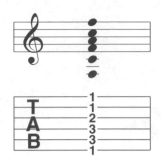

The F barre shape has its root on the sixth string. Move it up one fret and you get F#, up two and you get G. You can even play it way up at the 12th fret to create a barre chord of E.

B♭

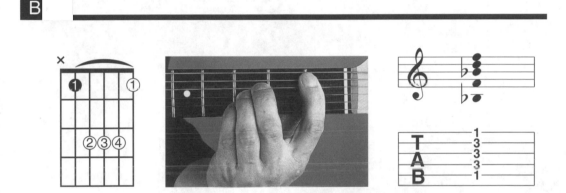

Any B♭-based barre shape has its root on the fifth string. Sometimes, if you're changing chords quickly, it's easier to change between the F and B♭ shapes because it involves less hand movement.

B♭   *'lazy version'*

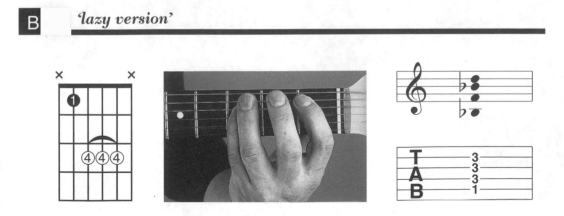

Lots of rock players favour this version of B♭– it sounds nearly as full, and is far easier to play.

Do make sure that you don't flatten the finger all the way over – the first string should not sound.

John Squire's guitar work with the Stone Roses in the 1980s featured lots of big, full-sounding barre chords.

Fm

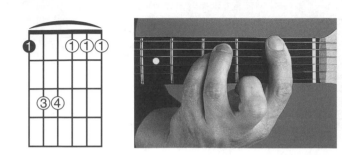

For this, the same principle applies as for the F major shape – move it up one fret and you get F#m, move it up one more and you get Gm, and so on all the way up to Em at the 12th fret.

B♭m

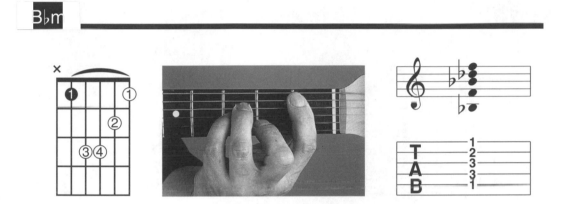

This minor shape has its root on the 5th string, so could create a chord of Bm if played at the 2nd fret, Cm at the 3rd etc. Its sweet tone makes it especially good for funk, jazz and dance music.

F7

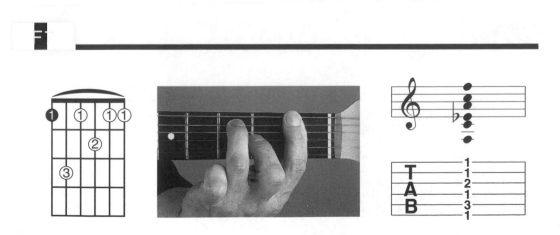

Although this barre version of F7 looks very similar to the ordinary barre F shape, it's quite difficult to make that barred fourth string sound clearly in the middle of the chord.

F7 (version 2)

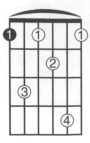

Add your little finger to the chord and you get this more colourful-sounding version of F7. It's a tricky stretch though, so ensure that all of the notes sound clearly as you strum across it.

B♭7

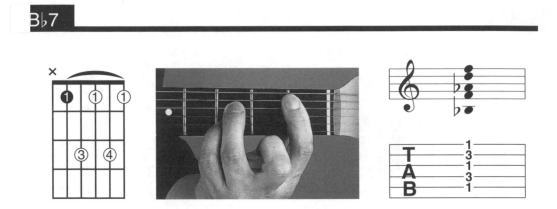

This is a barre version of the ordinary open A7 shape (see page 10). Note that the root is on the fifth string. This means that there's a chord of B7 at the 2nd fret, C7 at the 3rd, and A7 up at the 12th.

Fmaj7

Many players like to omit the first string when they play this chord because it clashes a bit with the note on the fourth string. Like all the other chords in this section, it can be moved to any fret.

B♭maj7

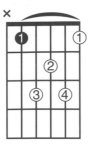  

This version of the major seventh barre chord is more common, and sounds 'sweeter' than the F shape opposite. Note that the barre doesn't have to press all the strings – just the fifth and first.

Fm7

Another six-string chord, this time with a barre covering all but one of the strings. Some funk players choose a 'partial chord' version, just using the first finger flattened over the first three strings.

B♭m7

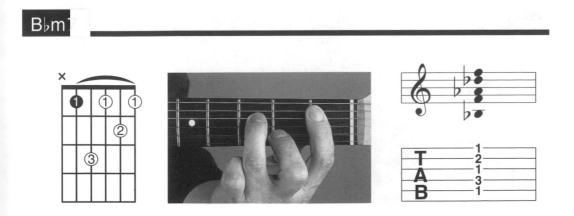

This difficult but versatile chord shape sounds just as good at the 13th fret as it does at the 1st.

Try sliding into it as you strum rhythmic patterns for a funky 1970s disco sound.

5

Power Chords

Power chords (also called '5' chords) are the sound behind almost every rock and metal band ever, from Black Sabbath to Metallica. They have a strident, aggressive feel, and sound good with lots of distortion (try comparing an F5 power chord and an F major with the overdrive levels cranked right up – the F5 wins every time). As with the barre chords in the previous sec-

tion, the F and B♭ versions of the chords can be moved up to any fret using the fingerboard diagrams on page 18. However, there are some great examples which feature open strings, and I've included these too. Power chords are also useful for making up your own rock riffs – try moving the chord around the neck while you play downstrokes on the bass strings with the plectrum.

F5

With this moveable power chord there are two choices – either play the three bass strings as shown, or only hit the sixth and fifth strings. Remember to mute the other three strings.

B♭5

Sometimes you may not need to move the F5 shape all over the neck – there may be a version of the power chord you want with its root on the fifth string.

A5

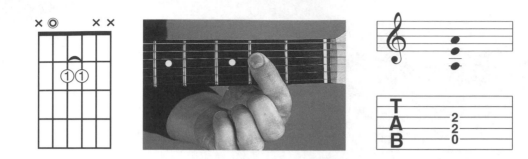

This open power chord appears at the beginning of *Won't Get Fooled Again* by The Who, *Tie Your* *Mother Down* by Queen, plus many a pub blues standard. It's a stripped-down version of A major.

A5 (version 2)

This version of A5 covers three octaves, so it has an even more powerful sound. If you have trouble flattening the little finger over two strings, do persevere – the effort will be worth it!

C5

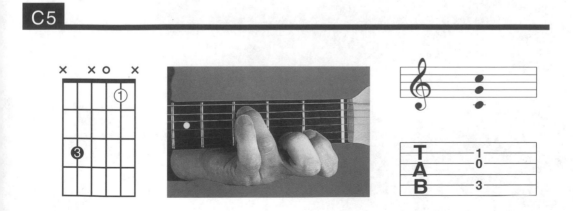

Although this is not a commonly-used shape, it's interesting because it uses muting techniques to stop some strings from sounding. Famously used in ZZ Top's *Gimme All Your Lovin'*.

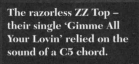
The razorless ZZ Top – their single 'Gimme All Your Lovin' relied on the sound of a C5 chord.

D5

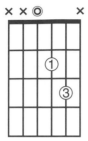  

Like the open A5 on page 25, this is just a simplified version of the equivalent major chord.

You might find, though, that a fretted version (B♭5 shape at the 5th fret) sounds more convincing.

D5 (version 2)

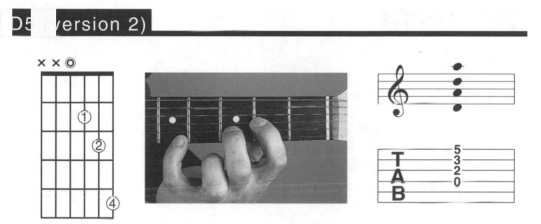

Here's a more spaced-out version of the same chord. Try adding distortion and delay, then picking across the strings one-by-one for a typical rock-anthem-type guitar intro.

E5

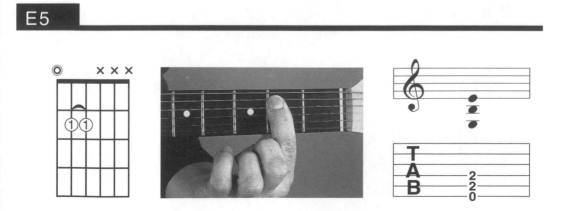

This is the lowest, thickest-sounding power chord anywhere on the guitar fingerboard. It sounds great played with downstrokes as a rock or blues accompaniment part.

29

E5 (version 2)

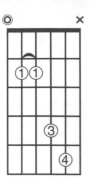

This is an expanded version of the more common three-string version (previous page). The first and second strings can, if so desired, be played open for a more 'jangly' sound.

F5 (version 2)

Although this version of F5 is moveable, its root is actually on the fourth string. So it creates G5 when played at the 5th fret, A♭5 at the 6th, and D5 way up at the 12th.

G5

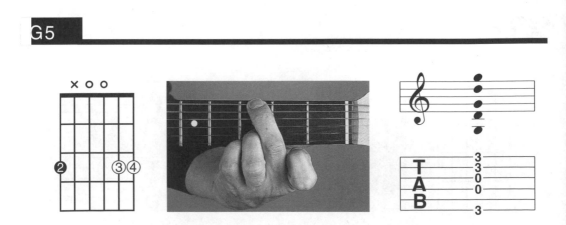

If you omit the 5th string from the easy G major chord shown on page 6, you get this powerful alternative to a G5 barre shape. Use the side of the second finger to mute the 5th string.

Tony Iommi of Black Sabbath wrote dozens of rock riffs by simply moving power chord shapes around the neck.

6

Suspended chords

Suspended chords are so-called because one of the notes has been taken out and replaced with a different note which isn't part of a major or minor chord – so a note is 'suspended'. What's more, they have an unfinished, suspended-in-space sound to them too. Sus chords, as they're known, comes in two types – sus2 and sus4, of which sus4 is the most common. They are rarely used on their own, because of their incomplete sound they nearly always 'resolve' to a more straightforward chord such as a major or minor. Check out the intro to Crowded House's *Don't Dream It's Over*, the strummed chords at the end of the chorus from The Beatles' *You've Got To Hide Your Love Away*, or The Who's *Pinball Wizard* (shown on page 44).

Fsus4

This is the standard six-string sus4 with its root on the sixth string. As with all F type barre chords, it can be moved to any fret position using the fingerboard diagrams on page 18.

B♭sus4

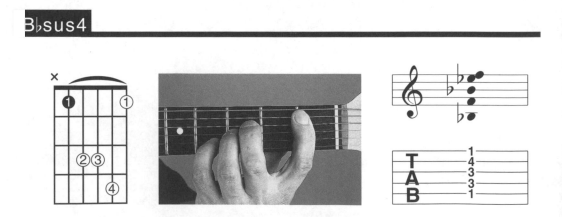

The other moveable sus4 shape has its root on the fifth string. Slide the little finger back one fret and you've got an ordinary B♭ barre shape, making the change from sus4 to major chord really easy.

B♭sus2

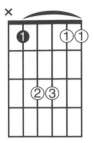  

If you play this moveable sus2 barre shape at the 6th fret, that's the intro chord from *Don't Dream It's Over* by Crowded House. Resolve this shape to a major chord by simply adding the little finger.

Asus2

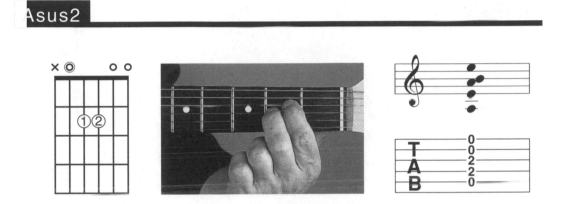

Much beloved of acoustic-playing songwriters, Asus2 sounds more complicated and difficult than it really is. Try making up riffs using combinations of A, Asus4 (see below) and Asus2.

Asus4

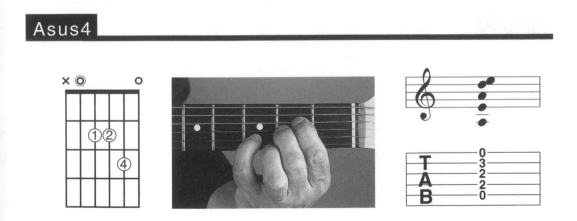

If you're playing a song that starts on a chord of D, wait until you get to a chord of A in the music, and try playing Asus4, followed by A. This is called a 'resolution' and is a useful songwriting tool.

Bsus4

The note of B (at the 4th fret, third string) is doubled by the open second string, creating a 12-string guitar effect. This shape appears in Suzanne Vega's song *Luka*.

Csus4

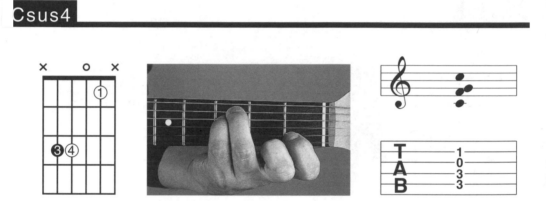

As long as you only play the middle four strings, this is a much easier alternative than the barre shape Csus4 at the 3rd fret. If you use this fingering, it's easy to resolve to a normal C chord.

Dsus2

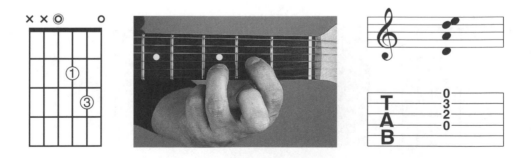

Play a D chord and take one finger off to create the chord of Dsus2. John Lennon used a combination of sus2, major, and sus4 chords like this to write *Happy Xmas (War Is Over)*.

Dsus4

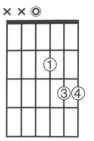
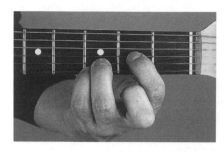
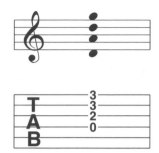

Many players like to keep their second finger at the 2nd fret on the first string (i.e. just one fret behind the little finger), in readiness for changing the Dsus4 back to a D.

Esus4

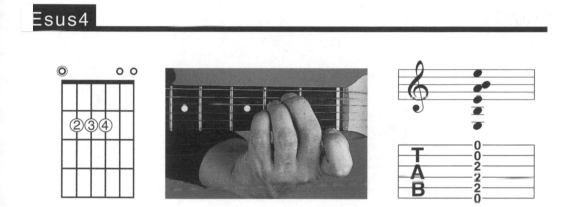

A similar idea can apply to Esus4, which resolves easily to a straight chord of E. Bear in mind, though, that including the open third string actually creates a chord of Em, not Esus2.

Gsus4

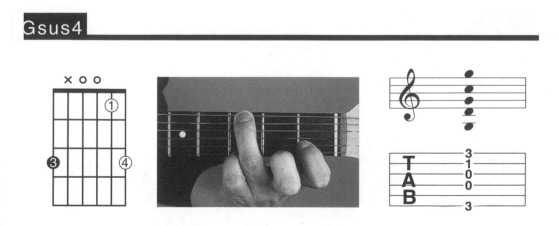

This less-used open sus4 chord is most useful if you're playing it on an acoustic, because it uses two open strings in the middle of the chord. Playing the first string is optional.

7

Other useful open chords

Sometimes, a particular shape or fingering might create a chord with a complex-sounding name, even if it's really easy to play. Shown here are some of the common examples you may see in songbooks. These shapes are particularly good for acoustic songwriting because they sound colourful and complex, helping to suggest melodies and ideas. All of these examples contain at least one open string, and none of them use barres.

You may notice that most of these examples are simply familiar chords with one or more of the notes replaced by an open string. You can apply this idea to almost any chord you know: experiment and see what happens.

Tip – if it doesn't sound good, try moving the whole shape to a different fret position.

Aadd9

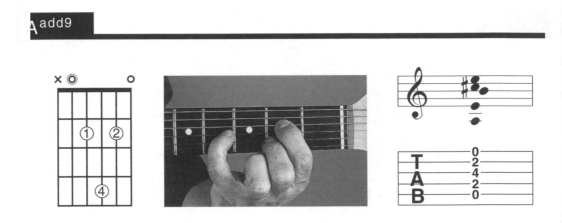

This chord is an adaption of the open A chord shape (see page 4), but take note of the finger number changes that are necessary to accomodate the stretch. It has a laid-back, 'Joni Mitchell' sound.

Cadd9

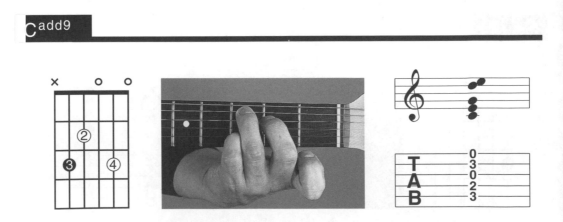

Much beloved of Noel Gallagher, this is a C chord with the little finger added at the 3rd fret. It works especially well with songs which start or end on a G chord. The open first string can be omitted.

Em^{add9}

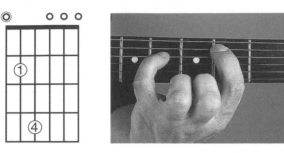
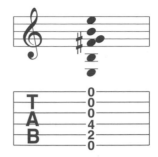

Although this chord isn't that great if you just strum it up and down, try picking across the notes one at a time – that clash in the middle of the chord sounds kind of 'heavy metal intro', doesn't it?

Fmaj7$^{\sharp11}$

Don't be put off by the jazzy-sounding name here – this is a great chord. Again, it's most effective when you pick the notes one at a time, but it can work with fingerstyle picking techniques too.

G6

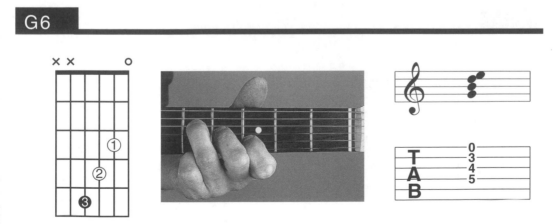

If you move the Fmaj7 shown on page 16 up two frets, you get this version of G6, as used by Keith Richards in the Rolling Stones' *Angie*, and at the end of The Beatles' *She Loves You*.

8

Slashed chords

Many chord books and song transcriptions feature 'slashed' chords, which confuses some guitarists because they don't know whether to play the chord on the left or the right of the slash. Here's how they work – the bit before the slash refers to the chord name itself; and the bit after is simply a single bass note. So A/G, for example, means a chord of A with a note of G in the bass. If you're playing in a band, it's normally OK for the guitarist to play the chord before the slash and the bass player to play the single bass note. If you're playing unaccompanied, you need to figure out a way to finger the chord *and* bass note; I've shown some examples here. Remember, any chord can have an alternative bassnote – try figuring out some of your own.

A/G

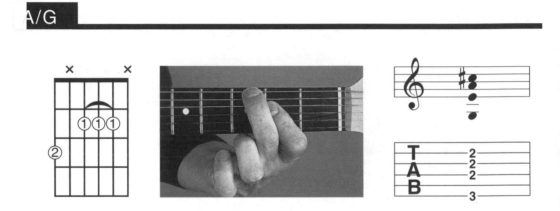

Although it's possible to play a straight A chord in the normal way and reach across with the little finger for the bass note, this version, with the first finger flattened across three strings, is much easier.

D/F#

Some guitar teachers will give you a slap on the wrist for hanging your thumb over the top of the neck like this, but Jimi Hendrix, Paul Simon and dozens of folk players can't all be wrong...

G/A

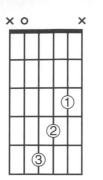  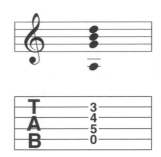

Of course, there's no reason why the bassnote shouldn't be an open string. The chord of G/A is sometimes referred to as A11, and it has a very warm, jazzy sound.

C/B

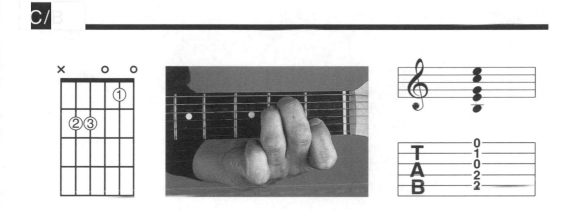

Here, the root note of an ordinary C chord has simply been dropped down a fret. Paul Simon uses it in the acoustic rhythm part from Simon & Garfunkel's hit *America*.

D/C

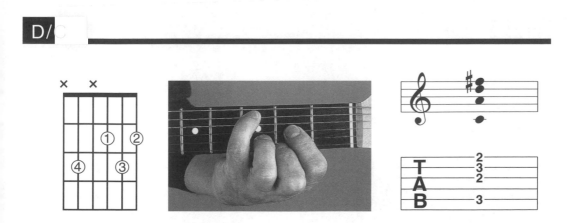

As with the A/G (opposite page), the side of the little finger is used to stop an open string from sounding. It's the second chord in the verse of The Beatles' *Dear Prudence*.

39

Playing a rhythm part doesn't always mean using the shapes you'll find in a chord encyclopaedia. Lots of pro players use less conventional shapes, either because they work better in the context of a band mix; because they're more convenient to play at the time; or simply because they prefer the sound. Here, I've shown two moveable chords which chord books sometimes miss out, plus three examples of 'partial chords'. Basically, a partial chord simply means missing out some of the notes of the chord – usually the lower ones in the bass range. Players as diverse as Nile Rogers of Chic, Prince, Steve Craddock of Ocean Colour Scene, or Eric Clapton have all used partial chords at one time or another. Any chord can be played as a partial shape.

D7 'Middle D7'

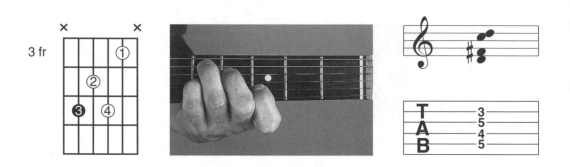

So-called because it doesn't use the outer two strings, this fretted shape is handy in many different styles, though it's perhaps most common in Rock 'n' Roll or Rhythm & Blues.

D 'Folky C shape'

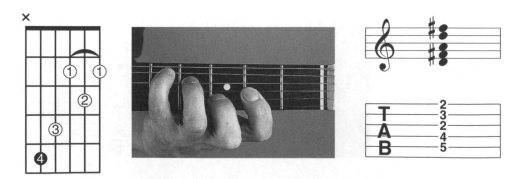

If you look carefully you'll notice that this is just a C chord moved up two frets, with a barre over the first three strings. Many players actually prefer this version to a conventional barre chord shape.

F (partial)

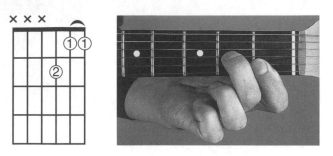 

The simplest way to create a partial chord is to look at any chord you already know – and don't play all of the notes. This is a chord of F with some of the lower notes removed.

Dm (partial)

This chord is based on a Dm barre at the 5th fret, but because you're not playing any of the bass notes, you don't need the barre. Try playing this shape while someone else plays an ordinary Dm.

A7 (partial)

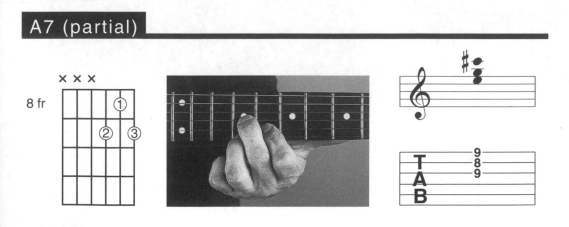

Although this isn't based on a conventional barre chord, it's still a valid seventh chord shape – it's basically an open D7 chord (as shown on page 11), moved up 7 frets.

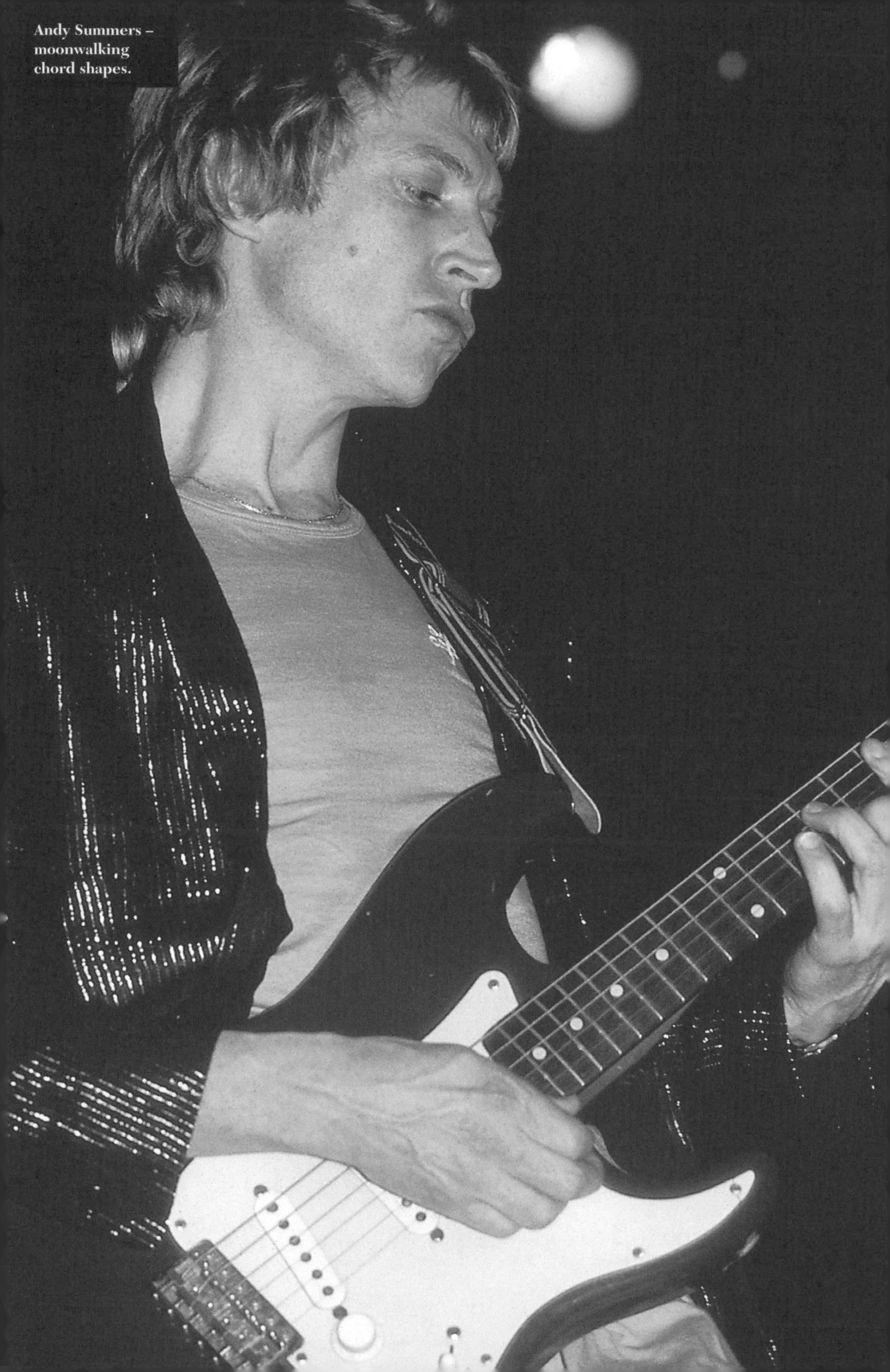
Andy Summers – moonwalking chord shapes.

There is a small number of chords that have become classics in their own right because they're instantly recognisable. The fourteen examples shown here have all been associated with a particular song, and some have been the subject of much debate among guitarists as to how they should be played!

Each of them should be identifiable if you just strum across the whole chord once, with the exception of the Chuck Berry example, which will need repeated up and down strumming.

Don't be put off by the fact that many of these chords have complex-sounding theoretical names – people are far more likely to know a chord as 'the end bit of James Bond' than they are to care about it being called E minor (major 9th)!

G7sus4/A — 'A Hard Day's Night'

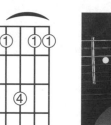 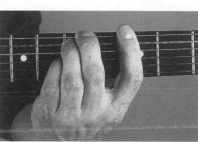 

This may sound slightly different from the Beatles' record because it was originally played on an electric 12-string. Nevertheless, this is how George Harrison played it, back in 1964.

Dm7add11 — 'Walkin' On The Moon'

This Police song would not have been complete without the 'chang' of this great-sounding chord on Andy Summers' Fender Telecaster. Add a C barre chord and you can play along with the bass riff.

Em^{maj9} '007'

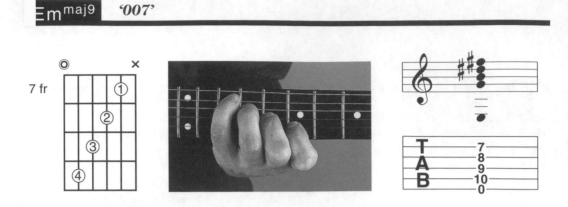

The James Bond Theme ends with this ominous-sounding chord, played in 1960 by session guitarist Vic Flick. Use the side of the fretting hand's first finger to mute the first string.

E7^{#9} '*The Hendrix chord*'

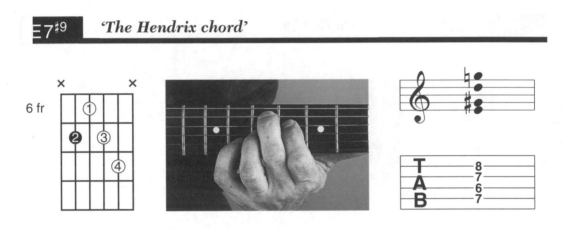

Foxy Lady, Purple Haze, Voodoo Chile… All three of these Jimi Hendrix classics have featured this chord. The open first and sixth strings are optional in each case, making the chord sound fuller.

Daug '*No Particular Place To Go*'

This partial chord, played up and down rapidly a total of 13 times, forms the intro to Chuck Berry's famous rock 'n' roll tune. The rest of the song uses chords of G7, C7 and D7.

44

Cmaj7   '*Design For Life*'

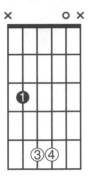  

Pick across the strings one by one, starting on the root note, until you get to the second string, then pick back in the other direction. It's the first part of the Manic Street Preachers' *Design For Life*.

D & Dsus4   '*Crazy Little Thing Called Love*'

 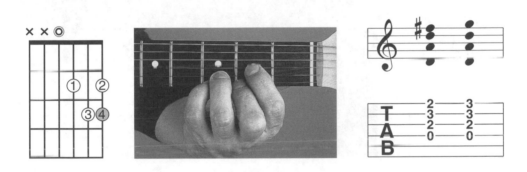

Play a normal D chord , then add and remove the little finger at the third fret (shown in grey) while you're strumming. That's the intro to this Queen single, from their 1980 album 'The Game'.

E/D   '*Hole Hearted*'

Play a D chord twice, then slide it up two frets and pick the strings one by one. Nuno Bettencourt plays this on an acoustic just before the verse section from Extreme's hit *Hole Hearted*.

E5   *'Paranoid'*

Because of the partial barre behind two of the fretted notes, you can play hammer-ons between the 7th and 9th fret, as Tony Iommi does in the intro from this early Black Sabbath recording.

E9   *'James Brown'*

This funky ninth chord shape appears in a long list of James Brown tunes, and is one of the most commonly-used chords in '70s funk and disco. Try sliding up to the chord as you strum rapidly.

Bsus4 & B   *'Pinball Wizard'*

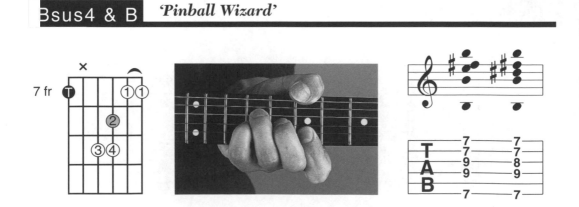

You need to reach the thumb over the top of the neck to reach the bass note here. Use fast up and down strums while you add and remove the little finger note at the 9th fret.

C#5^{add9}   *'Message In A Bottle'*

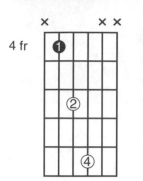

Here's another chord from a Police track. Most of the time, when 5add9 type chords appear in a song, they're picked one note at a time rather than strummed right across.

A & D/A   *'All Right Now'*

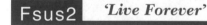

The D/A shape is played after a straight A chord in one of Paul Kossoff's guitar parts from this track by '70s rock-blues band Free. It also appears in Queen's *Hammer To Fall*.

Fsus2   *'Live Forever'*

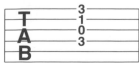

At the end of the chorus from this early Oasis hit, Noel Gallagher cranks up the distortion levels as he picks out a riff using the notes from this open chord shape.

James Dean Bradfield
of the Manic Street
Preachers –
Design For Cmaj7.

In my experience as a guitar examiner and teacher, it has always amazed me that so many candidates find rhythm playing their weakest area. When you consider that your average working guitarist spends around 95% of the time playing chord accompaniment, it seems odd that some players only ever want to learn riffs or solos.

There are many styles of music – Rock 'n' Roll, Rhythm & Blues, Reggae, Indie-rock, Britpop, even some rock and jazz – where the guitarist hardly ever plays a lead part.

Listed below are some bits of advice to help you maintain and improve the standard of your chord playing. I've also explained some of the common naming conventions that musicians may use when writing out chord sheets or 'charts' for guitar players.

Rhythm tips

- Sometimes just two or three notes will sound better than a full chord.

- Arpeggio techniques – *i.e.* picking out the notes of a chord one by one in time with the music – can make a rhythm guitar part more interesting.

- In rock music, especially if you're using distortion, power chords usually work better than other types.

- When you're using barre chords, don't just move an F shape up and down the neck. You may find there's a B♭ shape which is easier to get to.

- If a string is marked with an X in the fretbox, it's very important that you don't play it, because it will interfere with the sound of the chord.

- If you get fret buzz in a chord, move the fingers closer to the next fret – that way you'll need less pressure to get the strings sounding clearly.

- When learning a piece of music from a chart, don't stop and pause every time there's a difficult chord change. Attempt the whole piece at a slower tempo so you keep the changes in time. The speed will come with practice.

- Play with other musicians and singers whenever you can – it's the best and quickest way to improve your timing, technique and chord knowledge.

Naming conventions

Because of the different styles of guitarists throughout the world, several notation 'standards' have evolved. Below are several examples, all shown with a root note of C. On the left is printed the way you'll see chords in this book (usually the most common), followed by alternative namings.

C	C major, Cmaj
Cm	Cmin, C–
C7	Cdom7
Cmaj7	CM7, C△, C△7
Cm7	Cmin7, C-7
C5	C$^{(no\ 3rd)}$
Caug	C+, C^{+5}, C$^{\sharp5}$
C7$\sharp$9	C7$^{(-10)}$, C7$^{(\flat10)}$

Finally, if you don't know a chord, there's usually one that you do know which will fit just as well. Here are a few tips;

- Chords ending in 9, 11 or 13 can usually be replaced with an equivalent 7th – *eg* if you don't know Cm11, Cm7 should be OK. If you can't play C9, try C7, and so on.

- In most cases, straight major or minor chords will work instead of 7ths or 9ths.

- Power chords (*eg* C5, A5 etc) can be used as a substitute for any major or minor chord, including 7ths, 9ths etc.

GUITAR

ON TAP!

Whatever style of music you play, whatever type of guitar you own, sooner or later you're going to want to 'play lead'. There are thousands of transcription books out there which feature solos by your favourite artists, with every bend, pull-off and pick-scrape lovingly reproduced, but what do you do when you want to make up your own solos and melodies?

You can, of course, go out and buy a scale book, but these really just function as a musical dictionary – they don't tell you how to apply the scales, or give advice on how your guitar solos are supposed to *sound* – which is what it's all about, right?

This book features over 40 of the most useful and exciting scales and positions that gigging and recording guitarists use. In addition, each scale includes a chord sheet – the idea is that once you've learned the scale, you can practise playing lead lines over the chords in order to hear how they sound in context. Remember, a scale only becomes worth listening to when *you* make a great solo out of it!

Diagrams explained

Fretboxes

Fretboxes show the guitar upright i.e. with the headstock, nut and tuning pegs at the top of the picture – six vertical lines represent the strings.

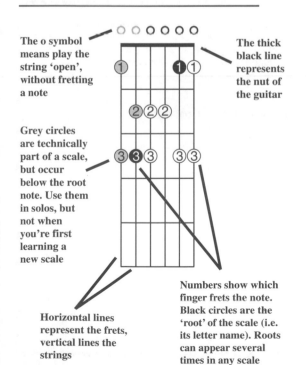

The o symbol means play the string 'open', without fretting a note

The thick black line represents the nut of the guitar

Grey circles are technically part of a scale, but occur below the root note. Use them in solos, but not when you're first learning a new scale

Horizontal lines represent the frets, vertical lines the strings

Numbers show which finger frets the note. Black circles are the 'root' of the scale (i.e. its letter name). Roots can appear several times in any scale

Notation and tablature

'Tab' is drawn with the guitar on its side, with the thickest string at the bottom – six horizontal lines represent the strings.

The top stave shows the scale as it would appear in traditional music notation

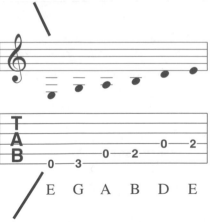

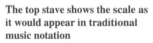

Below is the tablature – the numbers represent the fret positions. A zero means the string should be played open. The letters underneath the tab are the actual note names you're playing.

Many guitarists think they 'know' scales, sitting down and diligently learning all seven modes, for example, only to fall back on a couple of easy blues licks as soon as they play live.

Think of a scale as a set of notes which can be used to play a melody. That means that your lead part can contain any note from that scale, but it doesn't have to contain all of them, and they can be in any order.

When you practise a new scale, try to visualise it as a shape rather than as a long string of notes – this will help you to avoid playing boring, rambly solos, and allow you to improvise freely.

The most important technique is to pick the right scale in the first place. Generally, major-type scales (e.g. major, major pentatonic, 'country') sound better in major keys, and minor-type scales (e.g. minor, harmonic minor, minor pentatonic) sound better in minor keys. This simple rule works most of the time, but if it doesn't – experiment!

Finally, teach your ear as well as your fingers. Your aim is to be so familiar with a scale that you know how the lead line is going to sound *before* you play it. That way, you're playing the music that's in your head – this is true improvisation.

Practising

- All the scales in this book are shown ascending only. When you practise a scale, it should be played ascending and descending, without repeating the highest note.

- Play the scales evenly, so that each note is the same length. Don't speed up for easy sections and slow down for the more difficult bits. Use a metronome or drum machine, and fluency will develop naturally over time as you gradually increase the speed.

- Don't use any effects when you're learning a new scale. Distortion, overdrive and delay can fool you into thinking that you're playing better than you really are!

- Chord sheets are supplied throughout the book, each featuring chords which will sound good played as a backing for that particular scale. Record the sequence over and over again on tape, or get a friend to play the chords while you take a solo.

- Practise one scale at a time until it falls under your fingers comfortably.

Chord sheet – typical example

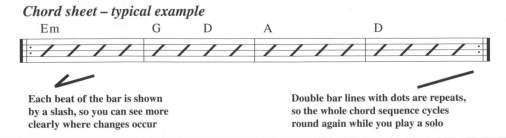

Each beat of the bar is shown by a slash, so you can see more clearly where changes occur

Double bar lines with dots are repeats, so the whole chord sequence cycles round again while you play a solo

A ny scale can be played in one of the 12 musical keys – it's simply a question of moving your hand to the right fret position, and finding the scale's root note on one of the diagrams below. Root notes (shown in black circles in the fretboxes) give a scale its letter name. Apart from the 'easy scales' chapter, all other scales in the book are shown in the key of A, but they can be easily transposed to any of the other 11 keys. So it's worth remembering that once you can play a new shape, you've in fact learned 12 scales!

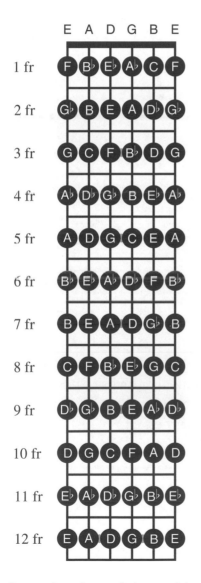

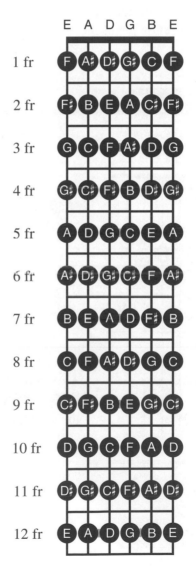

This diagram shows how to find any scale's root note, and will help you if the scale you want has a flat (♭) in its name.

This diagram shows the same information, but using alternate names for the notes. It will help you if the scale you want has a sharp (♯) in its name.

1

Easy Scales

As with chords, the first scales most people learn are in an 'open position', meaning they feature strings that aren't fretted. The advantage of these shapes is that they're easier to learn and can usually be played at greater speed. However, the open notes mean they can only be played in the keys shown, and some techniques (especially bends) are difficult in lower neck positions. Even so, the three scales shown in this section have been used by the likes of John Lee Hooker, Jimmy Page, John Squire and Noel Gallagher, so you're soloing in good company!

Em pentatonic

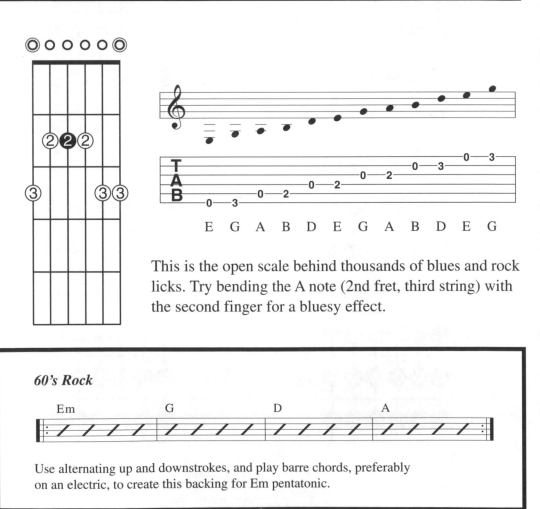

E   G   A   B   D   E   G   A   B   D   E   G

This is the open scale behind thousands of blues and rock licks. Try bending the A note (2nd fret, third string) with the second finger for a bluesy effect.

60's Rock

Em	G	D	A
/ / / /	/ / / /	/ / / /	/ / / /

Use alternating up and downstrokes, and play barre chords, preferably on an electric, to create this backing for Em pentatonic.

G major pentatonic

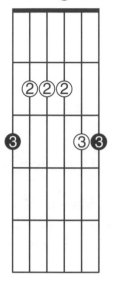

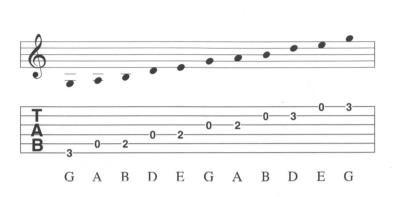

G A B D E G A B D E G

Major pentatonics have an upbeat, bright sound, and work well in country music, but you'll also hear them in folk, rock and jazz recordings.

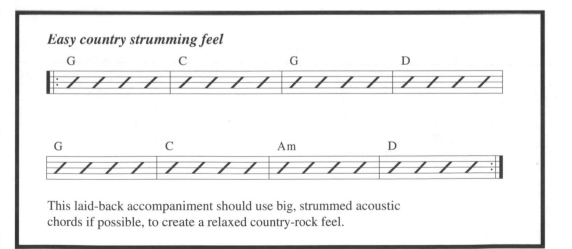

Easy country strumming feel

This laid-back accompaniment should use big, strummed acoustic chords if possible, to create a relaxed country-rock feel.

E blues

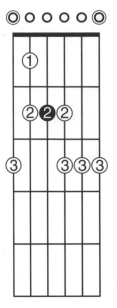

E G A B♭ B D E G A B♭ B D E G

The open E blues shape works over, er, blues in E!
Try not to linger on the B♭ notes too long because they
may clash with the backing chords at times during a solo.

Blues/R'n'B

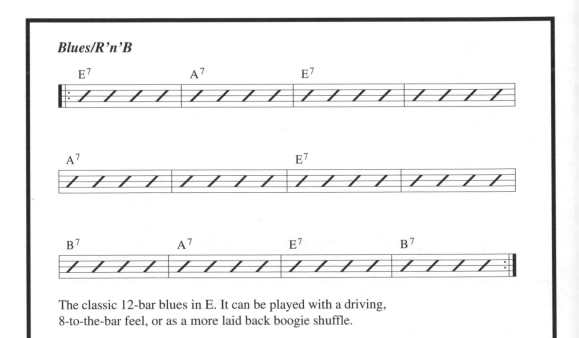

E⁷   A⁷   E⁷

A⁷   E⁷

B⁷   A⁷   E⁷   B⁷

The classic 12-bar blues in E. It can be played with a driving,
8-to-the-bar feel, or as a more laid back boogie shuffle.

John Lee Hooker has been using the E blues scale for over 60 years!

2

Pentatonics

The pentatonic scale has long been a favourite with guitarists. It's got it all – not difficult to learn, uncomplicated fingering, and sounds OK whatever you play! The vast majority of beginners never venture outside position 1 of the minor pentatonic (below) because it's the easiest, but as you can see there are lots of other shapes on the fingerboard.

The name means that there are five notes in the octave, and these represent the five notes that the human ear finds most pleasing, which is why it doesn't matter so much which notes you play.

You'll find the minor pentatonic scale in particular is great for making up rock riffs.

Just because pentatonics are fairly simple, don't think that professional players never use them. Clapton's *Layla* riff uses the D minor pentatonic scale. David Gilmour's epic solo in Pink Floyd's *Comfortably Numb* features runs taken from B minor pentatonic. More contemporary British artists have continued the tradition – Oasis, The Stone Roses and Kula Shaker have all used major and minor pentatonics.

Am pentatonic

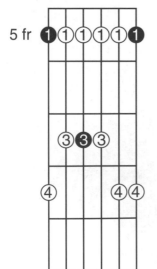

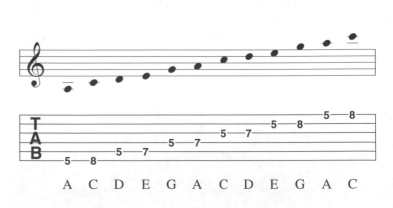

A C D E G A C D E G A C

This well-used but still hugely versatile box shape is the saviour of many a rock soloist. Try using hammer-ons and pull-offs between fretted notes.

Am pentatonic

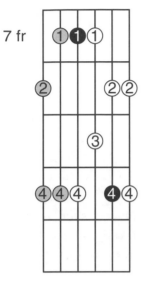

7 fr

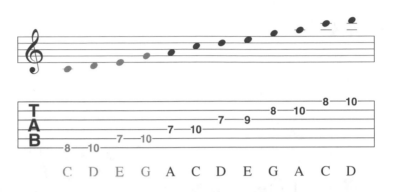

C D E G A C D E G A C D

Position 2 is a little more awkward, but it does have the advantage of moving further up the neck, which may present you with new improvising ideas.

Am pentatonic

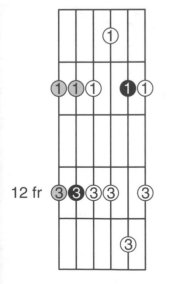

12 fr

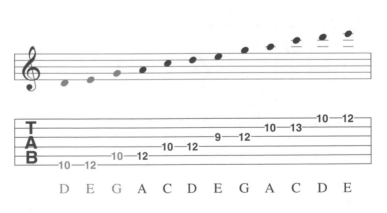

D E G A C D E G A C D E

Because of its two position shifts, few players use this shape in its entirety, but small fragments of it can be useful as you move to another position.

Am pentatonic

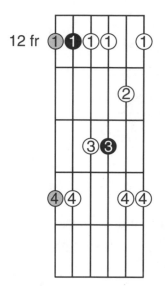

12 fr

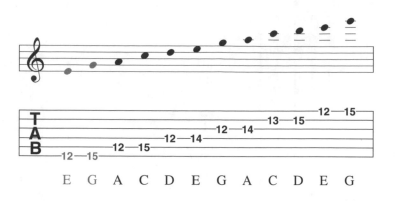

E   G   A   C   D   E   G   A   C   D   E   G

This shape is often favoured by blues players such as Gary Moore or B.B. King. Any note played with the little finger can be bent up a whole tone (2 frets' worth).

Am pentatonic

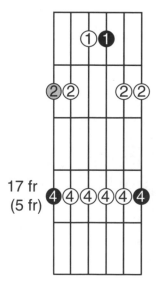

17 fr
(5 fr)

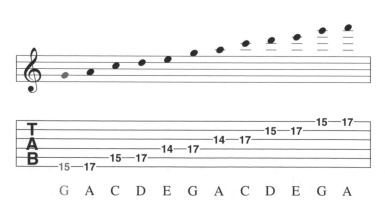

G   A   C   D   E   G   A   C   D   E   G   A

This high-altitude shape is perfect for squealy blues-rock moments too. Don't try the 17th fret position on an acoustic unless you're very brave – or very strong!

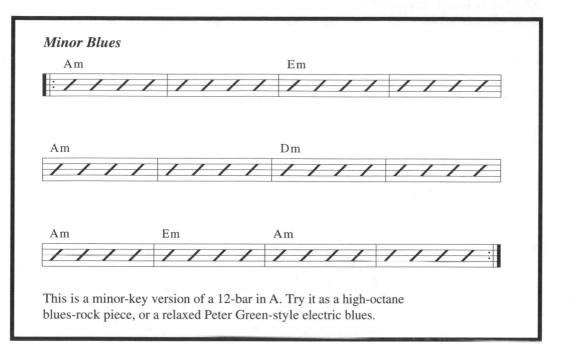

Minor Blues

This is a minor-key version of a 12-bar in A. Try it as a high-octane blues-rock piece, or a relaxed Peter Green-style electric blues.

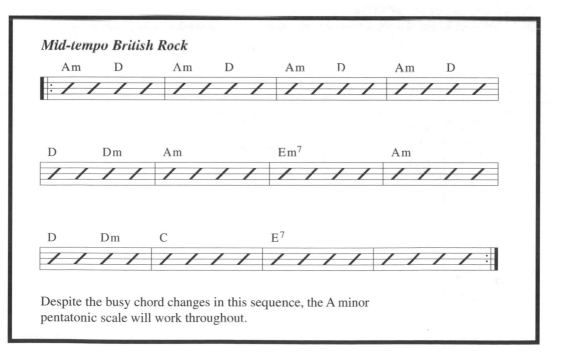

Mid-tempo British Rock

Despite the busy chord changes in this sequence, the A minor pentatonic scale will work throughout.

A major pentatonic

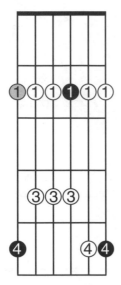

F♯ A B C♯ E F♯ A B C♯ E F♯ A

Although this looks very like the basic A minor pentatonic shape, note that it's played three frets lower, so the root note is played with the fourth finger.

A major pentatonic

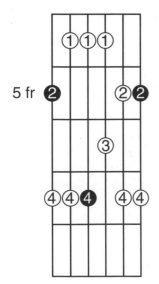

A B C♯ E F♯ A B C♯ E F♯ A B

This is a simplified version of the traditional major scale shape shown on page 22 – it just misses some notes out. Note that the root note is played with the second finger.

A major pentatonic

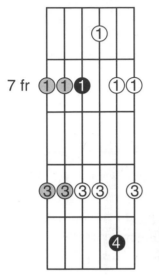

7 fr

B C♯ E F♯ A B C♯ E F♯ A B C♯

Despite some awkward position shifts, this pattern is well worth learning for the great hammer-ons and pull-offs you can do on the first two strings.

A major pentatonic

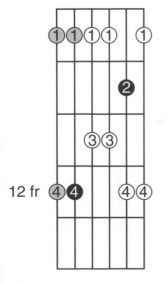

12 fr

C♯ E F♯ A B C♯ E F♯ A B C♯ E

This shape gets the second finger working, so you don't rely too much on the stronger first and third. Again, try pull-offs and hammer-ons at the top of the scale.

A major pentatonic

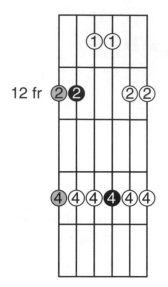

12 fr

E   F♯   A   B   C♯   E   F♯   A   B   C♯   E   F♯

This one might appear a little strange at first, but it's easier than it looks – just use one finger per fret throughout and the fingering should fall into place.

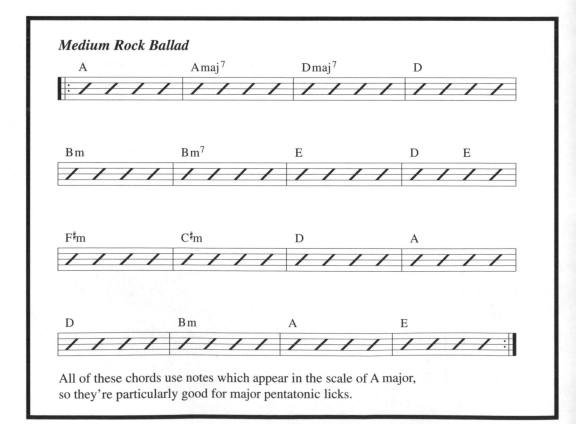

Medium Rock Ballad

| A | Amaj⁷ | Dmaj⁷ | D |

| Bm | Bm⁷ | E | D   E |

| F♯m | C♯m | D | A |

| D | Bm | A | E |

All of these chords use notes which appear in the scale of A major, so they're particularly good for major pentatonic licks.

Hendrix was mainly a minor pentatonic man, but also used major pentatonics and blues scale shapes in his solos.

A blues

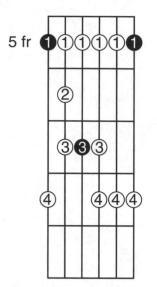

A C D E♭ E G A C D E♭ E G A C

Although the blues scale isn't strictly a pentatonic shape, it's included here because it's really a minor pentatonic box shape with a passing note added (the E♭ shown here).

A blues

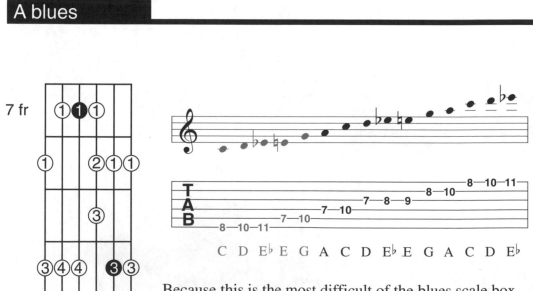

C D E♭ E G A C D E♭ E G A C D E♭

Because this is the most difficult of the blues scale box shapes to play, you may find it easier if some notes are played by sliding into position. Sounds good, too!

A blues

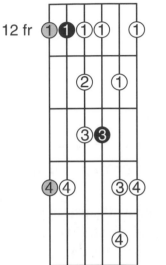

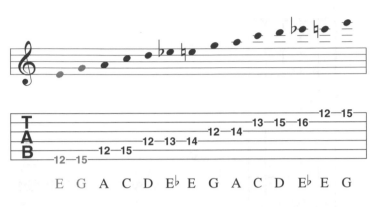

E G A C D E♭ E G A C D E♭ E G

This is the full version of the scale in this position, but many guitarists prefer to play it without the position shift by omitting the little finger note on the second string.

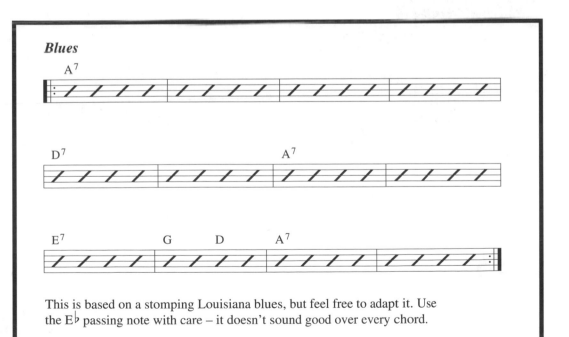

Blues

This is based on a stomping Louisiana blues, but feel free to adapt it. Use the E♭ passing note with care – it doesn't sound good over every chord.

A country

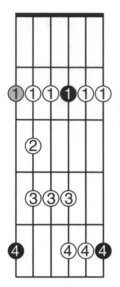

F♯ A B C C♯ E F♯ A B C C♯ E F♯ A

If the blues scale is a minor pentatonic with a passing note, this is the major pentatonic's equivalent. Practise the ascending scale with hammer-ons – you'll need them!

A country

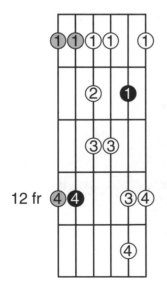

12 fr

C♯ E F♯ A B C C♯ E F♯ A B C C♯ E

The middle part of this scale shape is the most useful in an up-tempo solo, because it can be played at fairly high speed without a position shift.

Fast Fingerpickin' Country

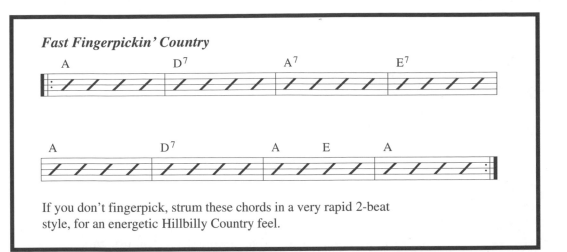

If you don't fingerpick, strum these chords in a very rapid 2-beat style, for an energetic Hillbilly Country feel.

When Chet Atkins ain't fingerpickin', he likes nothin' better than a barn-stompin' country scale solo line.

3

Major Scales

All of Western music – indeed, most of the world's music – owes something to the major scale. It provides the background for all musical harmony and theory. So it's perhaps surprising that guitarists don't use it more often.

The reason for this is that major scales sound very melodic and 'nice' – too nice, in fact, for aggressive genres like rock, metal and funk. But even if you are exclusively a rock player, it's still worth learning all five major scale fingerboard positions. As you learn new scales, patterns will begin to emerge which make reference to the major scale, and all of the modes have intervals and fingerboard shapes which are lifted from a major box shape. The major scale itself is also known as the 'Ionian mode' (see page 30).

If you use the major scale for soloing over chord changes, avoid playing too 'scalically'. It's all too easy to play six or seven notes from the scale in a row, and turn your epic solo into something that sounds like a piano student practising for their exams. But don't give up – major scale solos will put you in the company of George Benson, Hank Marvin, Nuno Bettencourt and George Harrison.

A major

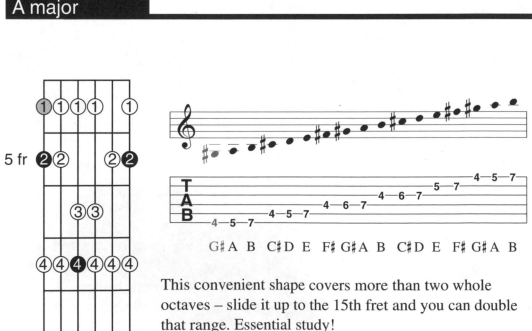

G♯ A B C♯ D E F♯ G♯ A B C♯ D E F♯ G♯ A B

This convenient shape covers more than two whole octaves – slide it up to the 15th fret and you can double that range. Essential study!

A major

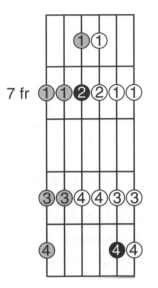

B C♯ D E F♯ G♯ A B C♯ D E F♯ G♯ A B C♯ D

Although lots of these notes are greyed-out (i.e. they're lower than the lowest root note) do explore this region of the shape – it's almost a whole octave.

A major

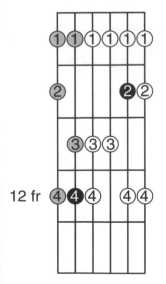

C♯ D E F♯ G♯ A B C♯ D E F♯ G♯ A B C♯ D E

You might like to think of this shape as being based on an open C chord fingering – the notes can also form the finger shapes for open chords of F, Am, Dm, and G.

A major

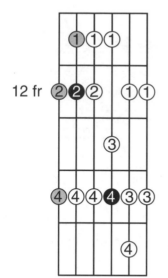

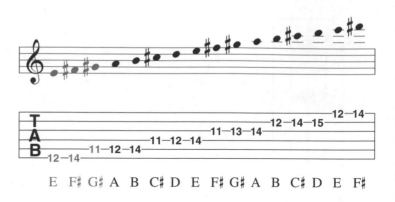

E F♯ G♯ A B C♯ D E F♯ G♯ A B C♯ D E F♯

Another position shift, but not a particularly difficult one. There are some opportunities to play double-stops (i.e. two notes on adjacent strings) if you re-finger this shape.

A major

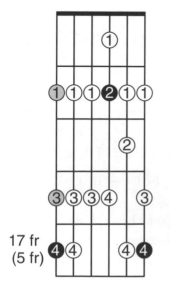

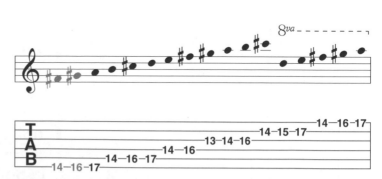

F♯ G♯ A B C♯ D E F♯ G♯ A B C♯ D E F♯ G♯ A

Like most of the shapes, this A major scale works in the position shown, and also 12 frets lower. This one's good for rapid playing on the first two strings.

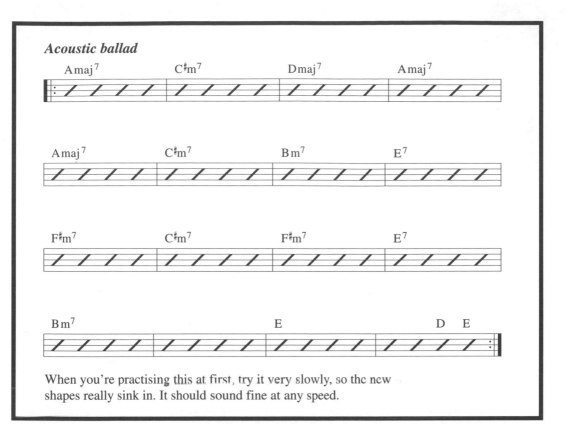

Acoustic ballad

When you're practising this at first, try it very slowly, so the new shapes really sink in. It should sound fine at any speed.

The ever-smiling Hank Marvin, no doubt contemplating yet another major key Shadows' melody.

4

Minor Scales

If you find that minor pentatonic solos have suited you thus far, you really should check out the minor scale. It contains all of the notes of the minor pentatonic, plus a couple more that can be used to expand the melodic possibilities of your lead lines.

As with the major scale, it's shown here in five positions (and remember that many of these can be played an octave higher simply by moving them up 12 frets). Don't feel that you need to follow every position shift exactly as shown here – in many cases, you'll be able to come up with good ideas simply by using part of one minor position.

Minor scales really only work in minor keys. Major chords may occur within a minor sequence, but the overall feel will remain minor.

When guitarists talk about minor scales, they mean the 'natural minor', also known technically as the Aeolian mode. It's not to be confused with the equally well-known (but far less versatile) harmonic minor scale shown on page 38. Notable minor scale guitar players include Mark Knopfler and Carlos Santana.

A minor

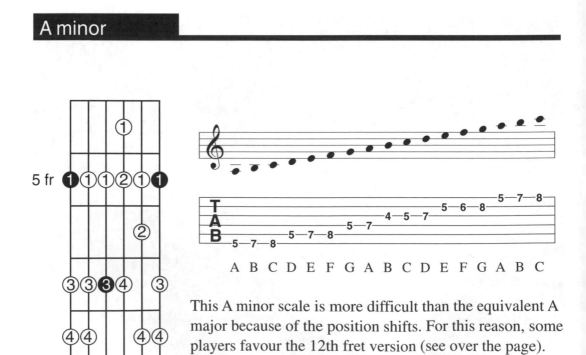

This A minor scale is more difficult than the equivalent A major because of the position shifts. For this reason, some players favour the 12th fret version (see over the page).

A minor

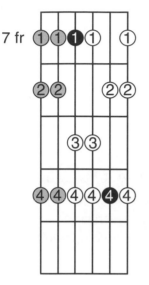

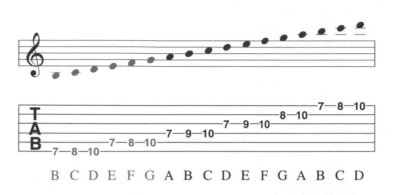

B C D E F G A B C D E F G A B C D

Minor scales work particularly well in this little-used position because you're using one finger per fret, which will enable you to develop speed much more easily.

A minor

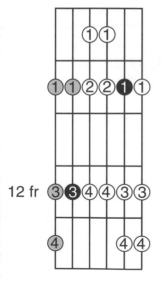

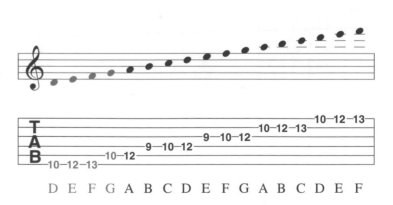

D E F G A B C D E F G A B C D E F

Playing the root with your third finger may feel strange, but it's worth practising so that you can play the lower greyed-out notes in a solo.

A minor

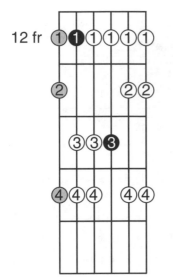

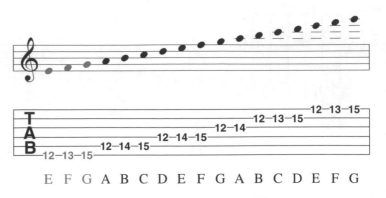

E F G A B C D E F G A B C D E F G

This is the easiest and perhaps the most versatile of the natural minor box shapes. Bend the top note up two frets' worth and you can get the high A.

A minor

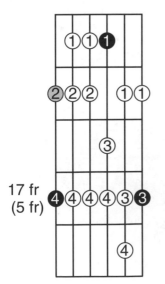

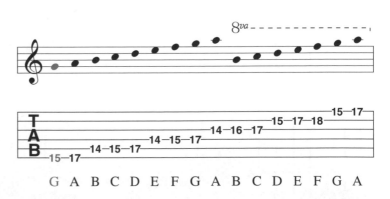

G A B C D E F G A B C D E F G A

Depending on which octave you choose for this position, you can get 1950's-style twang (5th fret) or mellow jazz-fusion tones (17th fret).

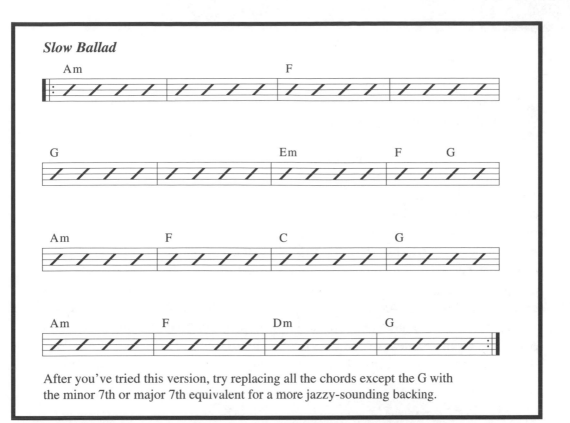

Slow Ballad

Am   F

G   Em   F   G

Am   F   C   G

Am   F   Dm   G

After you've tried this version, try replacing all the chords except the G with the minor 7th or major 7th equivalent for a more jazzy-sounding backing.

Mark Knopfler of Dire Straits – Minor for Nothin'.

5

Modes

Guitarists talk more rubbish about modes than they do about amp tone, and that's saying something! It's worth getting one thing straight right now – modes aren't any different from any other sort of scale. Like all scales, they all have a particular character, and like all scales, each mode is suited to specific chords or styles. The only reason they are in a category of their own is that they all come from the same (Ancient Greek) background, and so have appropriately exotic-sounding names. In rough order of importance for guitarists, these are;

Ionian, Aeolian, Mixolydian, Dorian, Lydian, Phrygian, and Locrian. As mentioned in previous chapters, the Ionan and Aeolian modes are just ordinary major and minor scales anyway, and it's best to think of the others as major or minor scales with a couple of notes altered.

In this chapter, you'll find all of the most useful fingerings for all but one of the modes. We've deliberately missed out the bizarre-sounding Locrian mode on the grounds that no guitarist has ever made a complete solo out of it. Well, not one that you'd like.

A Mixolydian

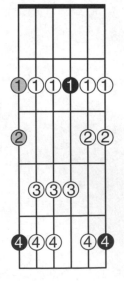

F♯ G A B C♯ D E F♯ G A B C♯ D E F♯ G A

The Mixolydian mode works particularly well in R & B styles, although it can sound 'Eastern' too (e.g. Led Zeppelin). It's just a major scale with a flattened 7th.

Crispian Mills, of Hindie-rockers Kula Shaker. Their debut album 'K' has the Mixolydian mode all over it.

A Mixolydian

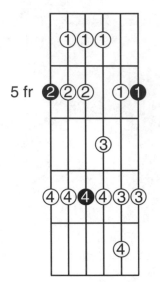

5 fr

A B C♯ D E F♯ G A B C♯ D E F♯ G A B

This position demonstrates the Mixolydian mode's similarity to the major scale. Compare it to the shape shown on page 22 – only the 7th note is different.

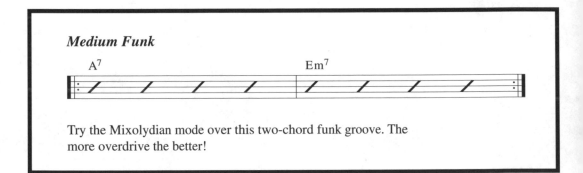

Medium Funk

A⁷   Em⁷

Try the Mixolydian mode over this two-chord funk groove. The more overdrive the better!

MODAL MYTHS
Guitar-shop-speak translated

"The Dorian's the second mode, so play it over D minor "

This may be true, but can be confusing if you're trying to learn what modes are all about. Like any scale, modes can be played from any root note. The Dorian is indeed a minor mode, but over a chord of Dm you could equally play a D minor scale, or D pentatonic minor, or D blues, for example, depending on the sound you want. The Dorian is a minor scale with one note altered – that's all.

"Play G Dorian, then C Mixolydian, then F Ionian"

The whole idea of modal harmony and melody is that you stay in the same mode – you don't keep skipping shapes every time there's a chord change. Modes can be thought of as musical keys in their own right, with their own chord sets and scales. Check out the chord sheets throughout this chapter to see examples of modal harmony patterns in a musical context.

A Dorian

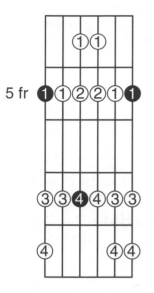

5 fr

A B C D E F♯ G A B C D E F♯ G A B C

The Dorian mode – or, if you prefer, a normal minor scale with the 6th note raised. We've shown three shapes for this extremely useful mode.

A Dorian

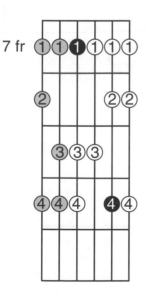

7 fr

B C D E F♯ G A B C D E F♯ G A B C D

This fingering-friendly box shape is often used in the rhythmic solos of the legendary Carlos Santana. The top note can be bent up two frets' worth.

A Dorian

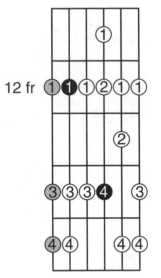

E F♯ G A B C D E F♯ G A B C D E F♯ G

If you don't like the position shift involved in this slightly more difficult shape, just re-finger the notes and play the top seven notes of the scale.

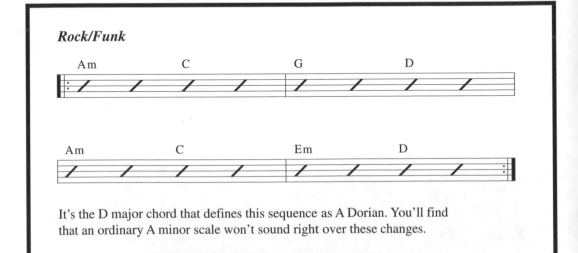

Rock/Funk

It's the D major chord that defines this sequence as A Dorian. You'll find that an ordinary A minor scale won't sound right over these changes.

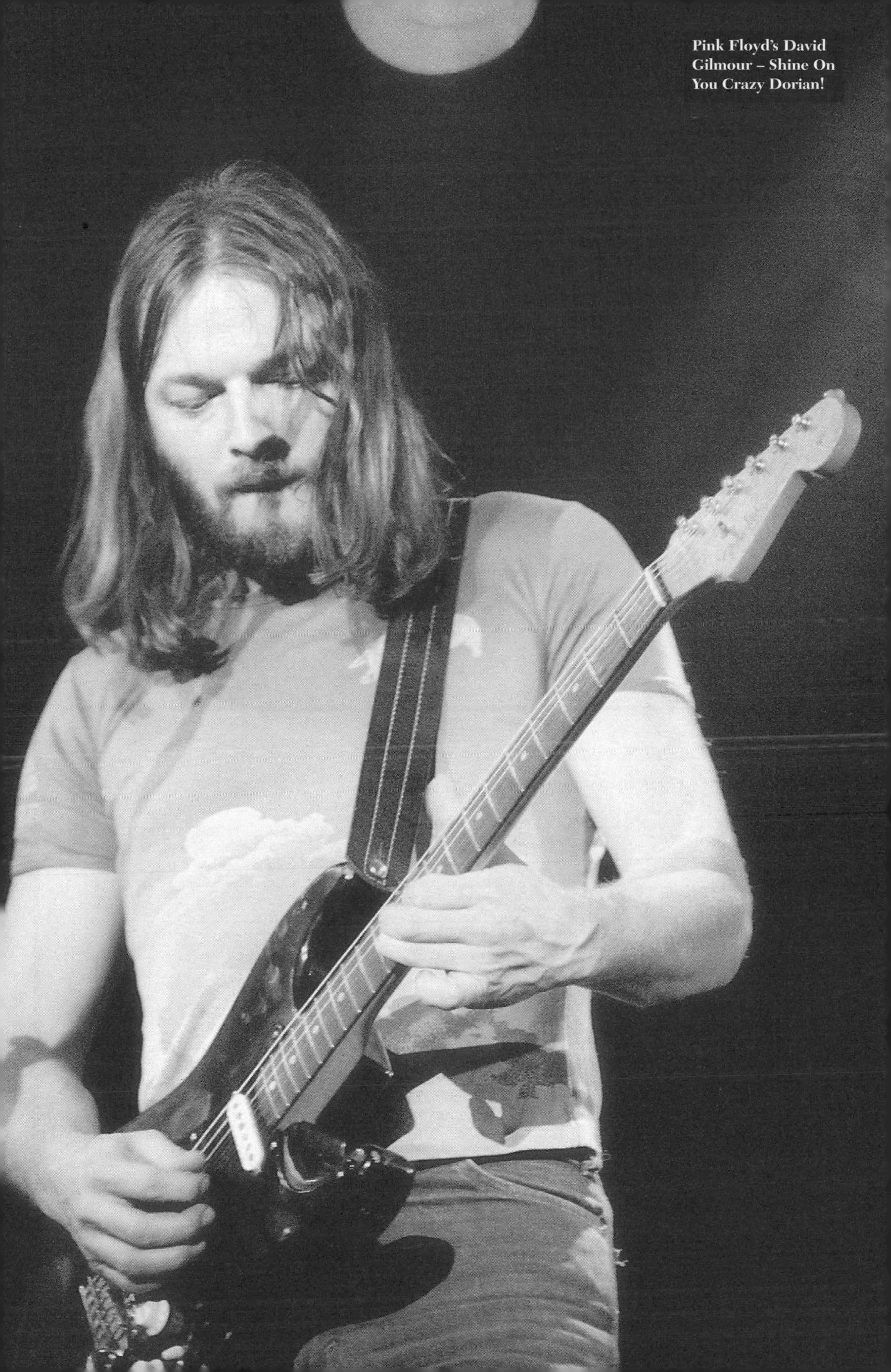

Pink Floyd's David Gilmour – Shine On You Crazy Dorian!

A Lydian

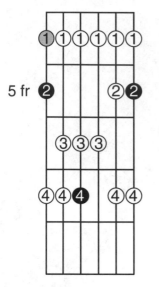

5 fr

G♯ A B C♯ D♯ E F♯ G♯ A B C♯ D♯ E F♯ G♯ A B

Think of the Lydian mode as a major scale with the fourth note raised by one fret – again, compare it to the major box shape on page 22.

Slow Lyrical Ballad

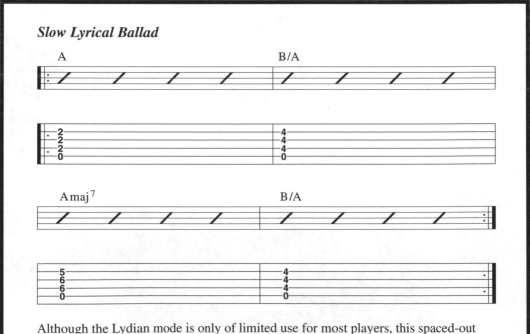

Although the Lydian mode is only of limited use for most players, this spaced-out sequence works a treat. Tab is included in case you don't know these chords.

A Phrygian

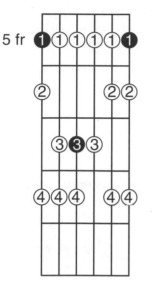

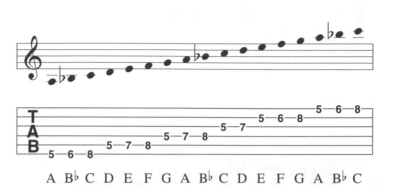

A B♭ C D E F G A B♭ C D E F G A B♭ C

Minor scale with a flattened second, but to you and me, it's that flamenco-sounding scale. It's almost impossible to apply this scale in rock and pop.

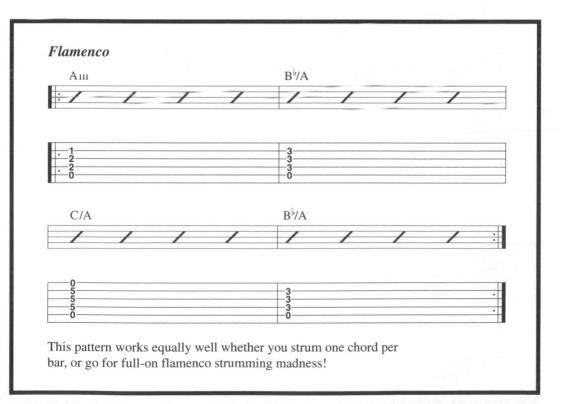

Flamenco

This pattern works equally well whether you strum one chord per bar, or go for full-on flamenco strumming madness!

6

Weird And Wonderful!

This chapter features a mishmash of some of the more unusual scales, used mainly by jazzers, and occasionally by rock players looking to spice up their solos. Some of them are not to be used throughout a solo – for example,

the harmonic minor scale's main function in guitar solos is to play over the 'five chord' – in the key of A minor, this would be a chord of E or E7. The melodic 'jazz' minor and 'altered' scale are also included as an introduction to jazz soloing.

A harmonic minor

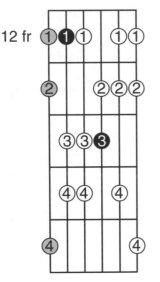

E F G♯ A B C D E F G♯ A B C D E F G♯

…also known as a minor scale with a raised 7th. If there's a chord change in a minor key sequence where the normal minor scale doesn't sound right, try this.

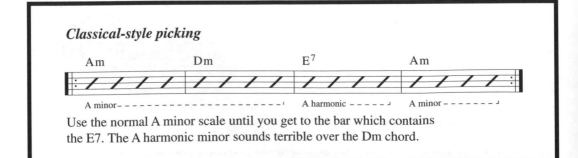

Classical-style picking

| Am | Dm | E⁷ | Am |

A minor- -ᴵ   A harmonic - - - - - ᴶ   A minor - - - - - - ᴶ

Use the normal A minor scale until you get to the bar which contains the E7. The A harmonic minor sounds terrible over the Dm chord.

A melodic minor

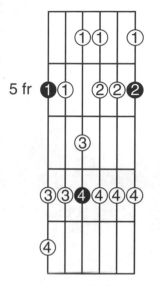

A B C D E F♯ G♯ A B C D E F♯ G♯ A B

If you take a major scale and make it minor just by flattening the third note, you get this curious beast. It instantly makes any minor solo sound 'jazzy'.

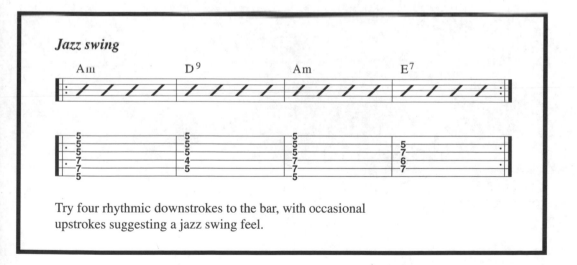

Try four rhythmic downstrokes to the bar, with occasional upstrokes suggesting a jazz swing feel.

Robben Ford says he borrowed his scale from BB King – how's that for a pedigree?!

A minor pentatonic major 6th

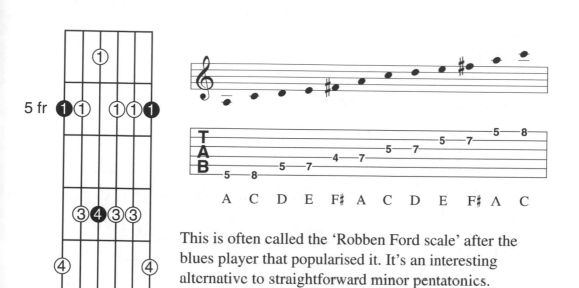

A   C   D   E   F♯ A   C   D   E   F♯ A   C

This is often called the 'Robben Ford scale' after the blues player that popularised it. It's an interesting alternative to straightforward minor pentatonics.

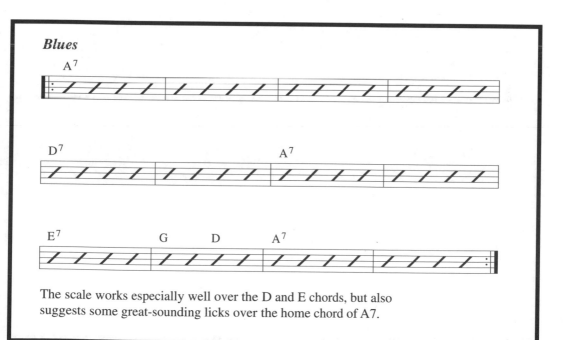

Blues

The scale works especially well over the D and E chords, but also suggests some great-sounding licks over the home chord of A7.

A altered

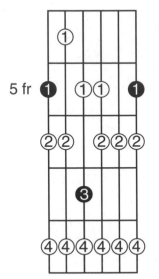

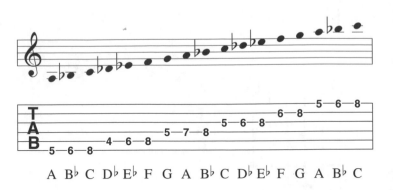

5 fr

A B♭ C D♭ E♭ F G A B♭ C D♭ E♭ F G A B♭ C

Just like the harmonic minor and diminished scales, this jazz favourite is mainly used over 'five' chords. Use it elsewhere at your own risk!

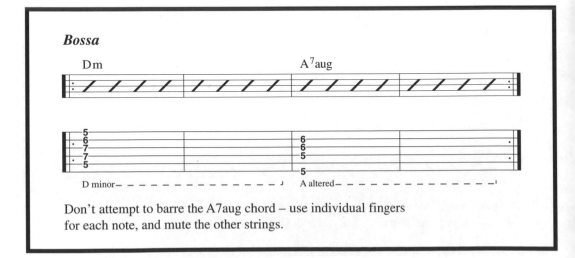

Bossa

Dm   A⁷aug

D minor — — — — — — — — — — — — ⌐   A altered — — — — — — — — — — — ⌐

Don't attempt to barre the A7aug chord – use individual fingers for each note, and mute the other strings.

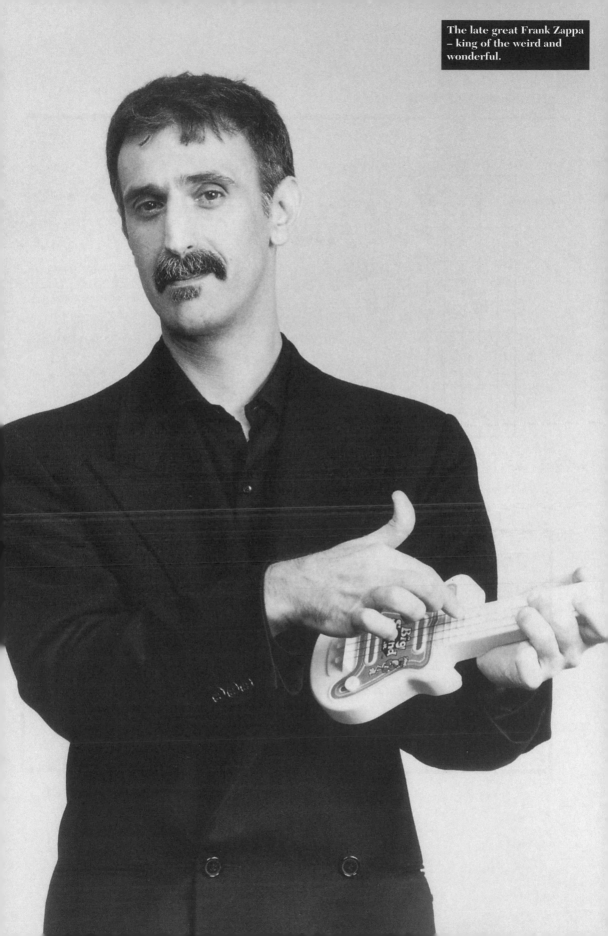

A whole tone

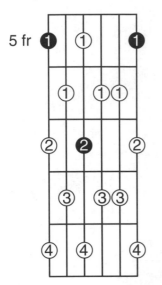

A B C♯ D♯ F G A B C♯ D♯ F G A B C♯

The whole tone scale means just that – i.e. the space between each note is two frets' worth. It's most effective when played over augmented chords.

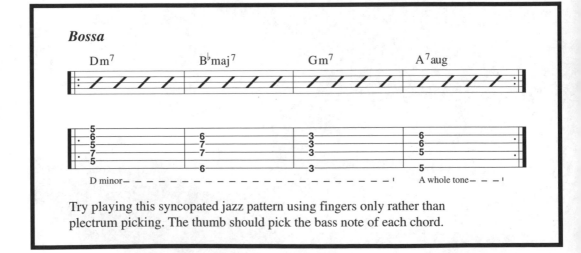

Bossa

Try playing this syncopated jazz pattern using fingers only rather than plectrum picking. The thumb should pick the bass note of each chord.

A diminished

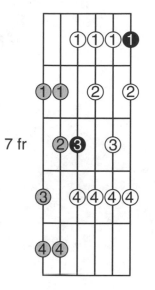

7 fr

B♭ C D♭ E♭ E F♯ G A B♭ C D♭ E♭ E F♯ G A B♭ C

Although you *can* use these scales over the relevant diminished chord, they're more common over the 'five' chord – e.g. in a D major sequence, this would be A7.

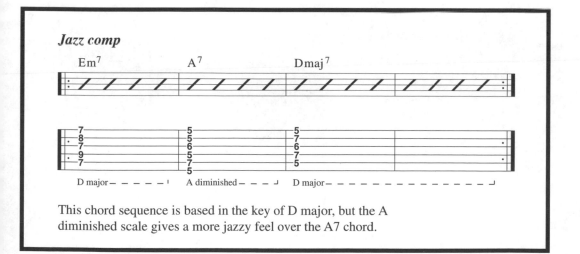

Jazz comp

Em⁷   A⁷   Dmaj⁷

D major — — — — —ꞁ A diminished — — — ⌐ D major — — — — — — — — — — — — ꞁ

This chord sequence is based in the key of D major, but the A diminished scale gives a more jazzy feel over the A7 chord.

Jazzer Pat Metheny knows his diminished from his whole tone.

Learning a new scale isn't the same as learning a new chord – you can't just go and use it straight away. It takes time to get used to its character, and to train your ear to recognise which of the notes work over certain chords. But learning a new scale, or even just a new position for a scale you already know, is a great way of getting your lead playing out of the musical ruts we all find ourselves in from time to time.

On this final page, I've supplied some hints and tips on how to turn your hard-learned scales into meaningful solos and riffs. But whatever you want to do with scales, keep this in mind; when I'm teaching electric guitar players, the most common mistake they make is to play scales far too fast, without really listening to the result. If your ear develops half as fast as your dexterity, you'll be well on the road to being a truly great musician.

Do...

• ...use phrasing. This means playing in musical 'sentences', so the solo can pause at the end of one phrase before it starts the next. Good phrasing gives the listener an opportunity to digest what they've just heard. Remember, the chord backing will carry on while your barrage of notes takes a breather.

• ...experiment with timing. Try playing a quick run of four or five short notes, followed by a couple of long, slow ones.

• ...use techniques. You can slide up to, or down to, any note of a scale. Try hammer-ons, pull-offs and vibrato to add interest.

• ...think like a singer. Once you've played a scale, sing a short musical phrase to yourself, and see if you can figure it out on the guitar.

• ...train your ear. Try singing a scale to yourself, then check by playing it back on the guitar to see how familiar you are with its character.

• ...play intervals. Why should your solo always go from one note in a scale to the next? Skip a few notes now and again.

• ...show off! If you find that a particular pattern of taps, hammer-ons or pull-offs helps you to play a scale pattern more rapidly, go for it!

• ...play round the chords. If one note of a scale doesn't sound right over the current chord, try another note from the same scale.

• ...emphasise notes that work well. If a note sounds great over any chord, keep coming back to it every time the chord appears again.

Don't...

• ...ramble. If you just play up and down the scale at random while the chords cycle past, the audience won't get an idea that there's an interesting guitar melody going on. As a general rule, if you've been playing for more than 4 bars without any rests or long notes, it's time to relax for a couple of beats.

• ...necessarily start solos on the root note. Just because you're playing in F#, say, it doesn't mean that the lead part has to begin on that note.

• ...over-use bends. Only a few notes of any scale will sound right when bent. Experiment to find out which these are for each new scale.

• ...use too many effects. The point of learning a new scale is to supply new melodic ideas, so don't blur these with loads of delay and fuzz.

• ...rely too much on 'licks'. These are previously-learned phrases that are played from memory. This will ultimately limit your solos.

• ...play 'scalically' all the time. Running up and down the scale, even at high speed, doesn't always create the most musical result.

• ...try to play too fast. Make sure every note of the scale sounds out cleanly and clearly at a slow tempo before you attempt anything flash.

• ...ignore the chords. If you don't think a note works over a chord, go back and check. Then you won't make the same mistake again.

• ...worry about breaking the rules. If you find a scale that doesn't appear in this book, but you like the way it sounds, use it!

When most of us pick up a guitar for the first time, we take it for granted that there is a correct way to tune the instrument. But there's no real reason that we always have to use EADGBE just because it's the first tuning we learn. Players have been detuning and retuning their guitars since the birth of the blues in the early part of this century. Indeed, if you go back far enough, even the guitar's 16th-century ancestors used altered tunings – the lute and vihuela, for example, were often tuned GCFADG.

And there is no shortage of contemporary players using tunings. A simple half-step drop (i.e. detuning the whole guitar by a semitone) was often favoured by rock and blues players like Jimi Hendrix, Kurt Cobain, Stevie Ray Vaughan and Nuno Bettencourt. At the other extreme, there are many totally unrelated tunings, as used by acoustic players like Crosby, Stills & Nash, Davey Graham and Joni Mitchell, or heavy metal acts like Korn.

Guitar Tunings To Go ! gives you an introduction to the most commonly-used tunings, and provides examples of how they can be used, with chord shapes for each new tuning. Once you've attempted these, try tweaking strings here and there to create new possibilities. You may even invent a tuning that no-one's ever heard of before. And if you do, make sure it goes in the next edition of this book!

Tuning tips

- Many tunings require the pitch of the string to be altered quite drastically. This can lead to broken strings (when the pitch is raised too far) or fret-buzz and poor tone (when lowered too far). For this reason, you may find that a new tuning requires a different set of strings. As a rule of thumb, if you have to alter a string's pitch by more than a whole tone (i.e. two frets' worth), you should really think about a different string gauge if you're going to use that tuning regularly.

- All the tunings in the book are shown relative to standard tuning (see right). However, you'll find it much easier to quickly and accurately retune a string if you use a chromatic electronic guitar tuner. These start from around £15.

- Some tunings will require a change in your technique in order to get the best out of them. Open chord tunings (e.g. 'Open D') generally sound good with big, wide strums, but some more unusual ones (e.g. 'All The 4ths') can be more effective with single notes or even harmonics. Of course, this can be a good thing too – a new tuning is a great way to get your playing out of bad habits.

- If you're an electric player, it is recommended that you try these tunings on a guitar which does not feature a floating bridge/locking trem system. Their fulcrum design makes tuning shifts time-consuming and inaccurate.

- If you're going to explore open chord tunings, you really should consider buying a bottleneck or 'slide'. They cost from £3-£10.

Diagrams Explained

Tunings

Shown in the middle row of each chart are the note-names of the strings.

The top row represents the string numbers (the 6th string is the thickest on a regular guitar.)

6	5	4	3	2	1
D	G	D	G	B	D
-2	-2	0	0	0	-2

The numbers below show how much the string has to be raised or lowered in relation to normal EADGBE tuning.

Fretboxes

Fretboxes show the guitar upright *i.e.* with the headstock, nut and tuning pegs at the top of the picture – six vertical lines represent the strings.

The x symbol means you should not play this string

The o symbol means play the string 'open' without fretting a note

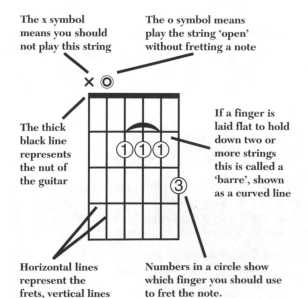

The thick black line represents the nut of the guitar

If a finger is laid flat to hold down two or more strings this is called a 'barre', shown as a curved line

Horizontal lines represent the frets, vertical lines the strings

Numbers in a circle show which finger you should use to fret the note.

Chord notation

Chord tab is drawn with the guitar on its side, with the thickest string at the bottom – six horizontal lines represent the strings.

The top stave shows the chord as it would appear in traditional music notation

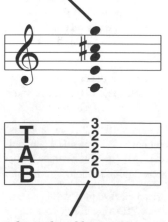

Below is the tablature – the numbers represent the fret positions. A zero means the string should be played open

Neil Young and his fellow country rockers, Crosby, Stills & Nash were responsible for some of the most extreme tunings of the 1960s.

6	5	4	3	2	1
D	A	D	G	B	E
-2	0	0	0	0	0

The simplest way to retune a guitar is to alter the pitch of the sixth string – these are referred to as 'dropped' tunings. Of these, the most useful is dropped D. Its most common usage is when you're playing in the key of D, because it produces a deep, resonant six-string chord from an ordinary D shape (see below).

Because only one string is altered from regular tuning, some of the open chords you already know won't have to change to suit the tuning; for example, C, Am, B7 and Dm are all the same shapes, but the Dm can also feature the two bass strings.

The low D bass note also provides new riff posibilities; you'll find that you can create rock riffs just by flattening your finger over the three bass strings and moving it around.

Famous users of dropped D include The Beatles, Manic Street Preachers, John Denver and James Taylor.

Tuning Guide

To get to dropped D from normal EADGBE tuning, you need to make sure the sixth string sounds exactly one octave lower than the fourth string. To do this, play the fourth string open (if you were in tune to start with, this will be a note of D) and gradually turn the sixth string's peg until the note sounds the same (some guitarists like to play a 12th fret harmonic on the sixth string for greater accuracy). As a final check, play an open D chord and strum all six strings.

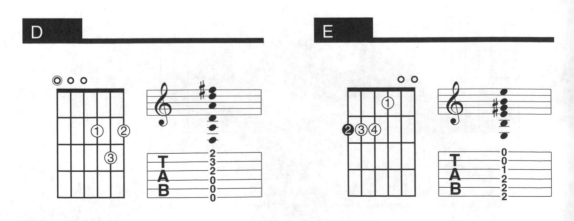

Basic chords

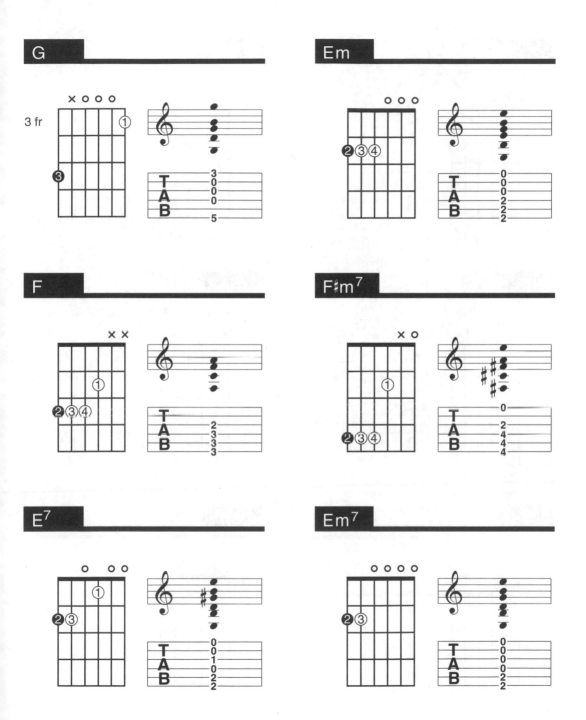

Because of the dropped bass note, any chords which had their root note on the sixth string in normal tuning will now have to be refingered. These are some of the most common versions.

D chords

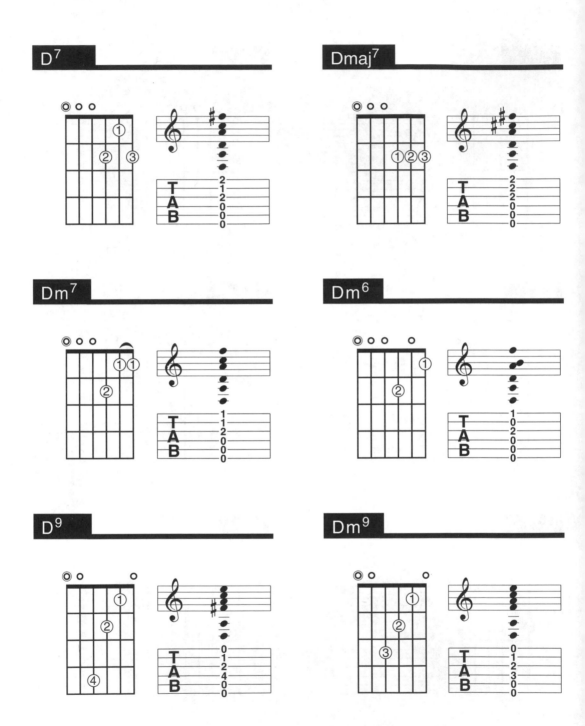

The compromises you have to make for some chords (see previous page) are more than worth it when you hear the great sounds that can be produced with that deep bassnote. All of these chords use six strings.

Further ideas

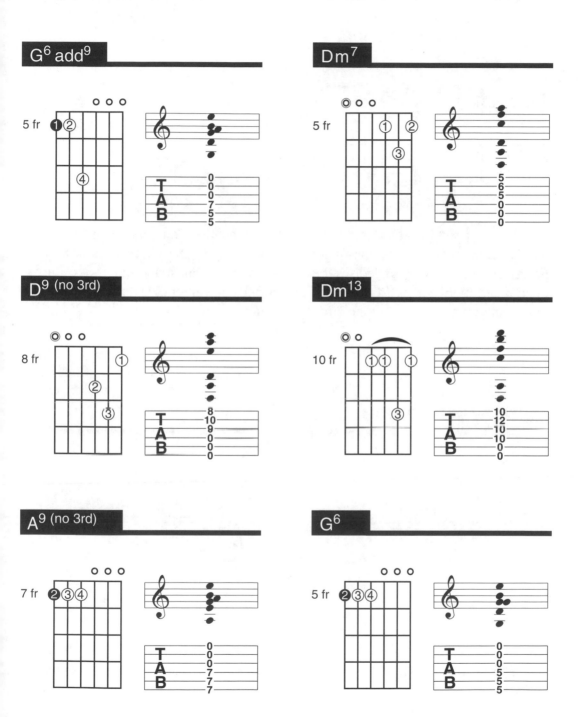

By using higher fret positions in conjunction with with altered sixth string, the above exotic-sounding chords can be created. Despite the jazzy names, these shapes are just as useful in rock and folk styles.

'Gimme 5'

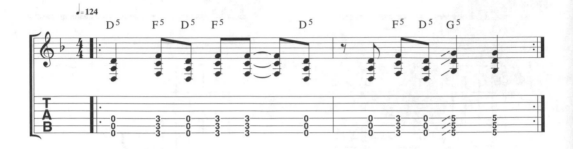

The dropped D bass note can be used to create very simple one-finger power chords. This example uses the open position, plus the 3rd and 5th frets, but you could also try the 7th, 10th and 12th fret versions when you're trying out your own ideas. This type of riff can sound like the Rolling Stones or Pantera, depending on how much distortion you use!

'Come Out To Play'

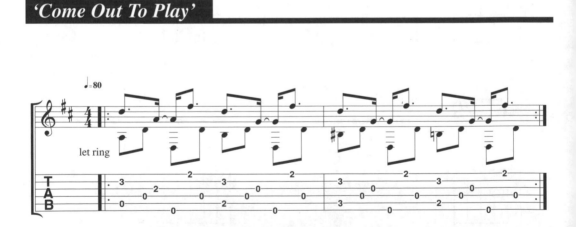

That resonant sixth string can also work well if used as a drone note in a fingerstyle part. This example features the thumb playing an alternating bass line on the fourth, fifth and sixth strings, with one finger each picking the first, second and third strings. The co-ordination can be difficult at first, so start slowly and gradually build up speed.

George Harrison learned
fingerstyle guitar – and
the Dropped D tuning –
from Donovan.

Double Dropped D Tuning

6	5	4	3	2	1
D	A	D	G	B	D
-2	0	0	0	0	-2

If you can drop the sixth string from its usual pitch of E to D, it stands to reason that you can do the same with the first string. Although this tuning isn't as common as dropped D, the possibilities it provides make it well worth a look, especially if you're interested in songwriting.

In this chapter are some fingerings you can use to create straightforward open chords, but as with most tunings, more interesting effects can be created when you play chords that are impossible in regular tuning. Try playing a normal C chord shape then taking your first finger off while you strum five strings. The resulting open Cmaj9 sound can't be reproduced in any other tuning.

The dropped first string is most useful in this tuning when played open, so try other normal open chord shapes (e.g. C, Am, Em) to hear how that open first string changes the sound.

Tuning Guide

Once you've got the sixth string detuned to D (see previous chapter), you need to lower the first string by a whole tone (two frets' worth). The first, and easiest way to do this is to fret the second string at the third fret, then lower the pitch of the first string until it matches the fretted note (there should be no discernible 'wobble' when both notes are played together). A slightly more accurate method is to play a harmonic at the 12th fret of the fourth string, and tune the first string to that.

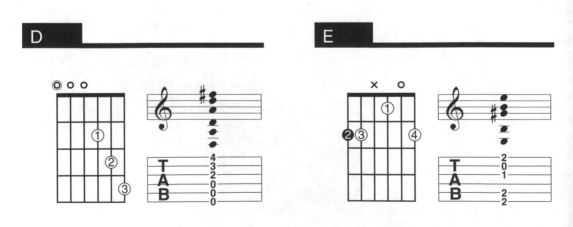

D

E

Basic chords

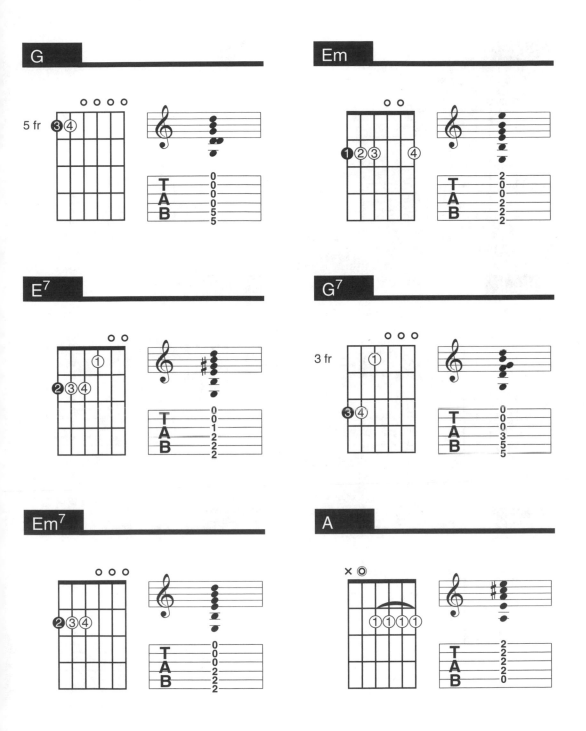

Most of these chords sound similar to their regular-tuned counterparts, but there are subtle differences. The G7 and Em7 are richer-sounding, and the open A has the added advantage of being dead easy to play!

D chords

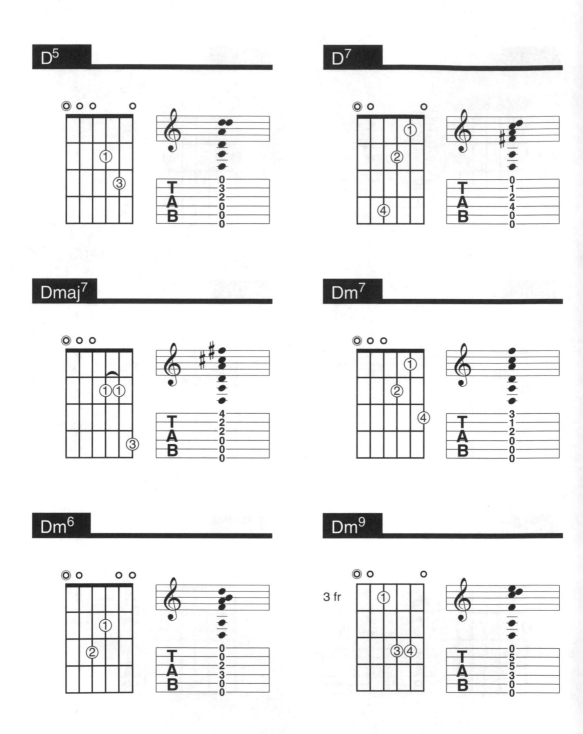

Here are six examples which have the sixth string D note as their root. The Dm9 uses the open string to create a cluster of three consecutive notes – great for arpeggios. Note the doubled note in the D5 chord.

Further ideas

Shown here are some other chords which use the open top D as an added note, plus three which use doubled notes. The 12-string effect is created using a combination of octaves and unison notes.

'AK-47'

Picking across an open chord while letting the notes ring on is a useful technique in normal tuning, but when you're in an altered tuning the results can be beautiful. This two-chord example uses the open D note to create a slight clash with the fretted chord notes. Don't be put off by the difficult sounding chord name in bar 2 – the shape itself is fairly easy.

'Widdly Diddly'

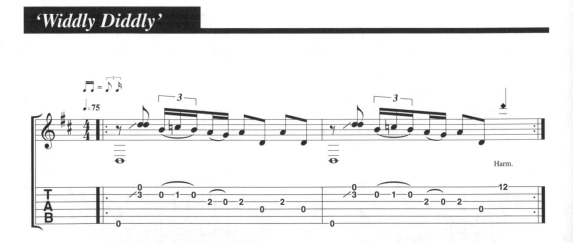

This folk-style acoustic riff makes full use of the tuning – bass note, open-note pull-offs, unisons, even a harmonic. The example suggests letting the bass note ring on throughout the bar, but it can be shorter, or even omitted entirely if you wish. As with much fingerstyle folk guitar, there are bonus points for being able to play it at a ridiculous speed!

Jimmy Page used many tunings, including Double Dropped D, in his Led Zeppelin days and beyond.

3

Open G Tuning

6	5	4	3	2	1
D	G	D	G	B	D
-2	-2	0	0	0	-2

This is the first open tuning we've looked at – that is, it creates a simple chord when you strum all the strings. This gives the player the advantage of being able to create any major chord simply by barring the first finger across all the strings (see below).

Some blues players refer to open G as 'Spanish' tuning, and more recently it has even been called 'Keef' tuning, because The Rolling Stones' Keith Richards uses it (albeit removing the sixth string from his guitar). However, it's also been under the fingers of folk players such as Joni Mitchell or John Renbourn, as well as bluesmen like Robert Johnson and Muddy Waters.

Like all open chord tunings, open G is used extensively by slide players. If you try the tuning using bottleneck, experiment with single-note and double-stopped licks as well as full chords – you'll be surprised how easily you can achieve classic blues effects!

Tuning Guide

To produce open G from regular tuning, drop the first and sixth strings to a pitch of D (see the previous chapter) to produce Double Dropped D tuning, then play the (now dropped) sixth string at the fifth fret. Drop the fifth string until its pitch matches that of the fretted note. Alternatively, play a harmonic on the 12th fret of the fifth string, and keep lowering its pitch until it matches that of the open third string. To check if you're in tune, just strum all the strings at once!

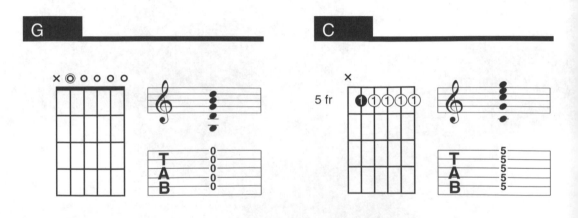

116

Basic chords

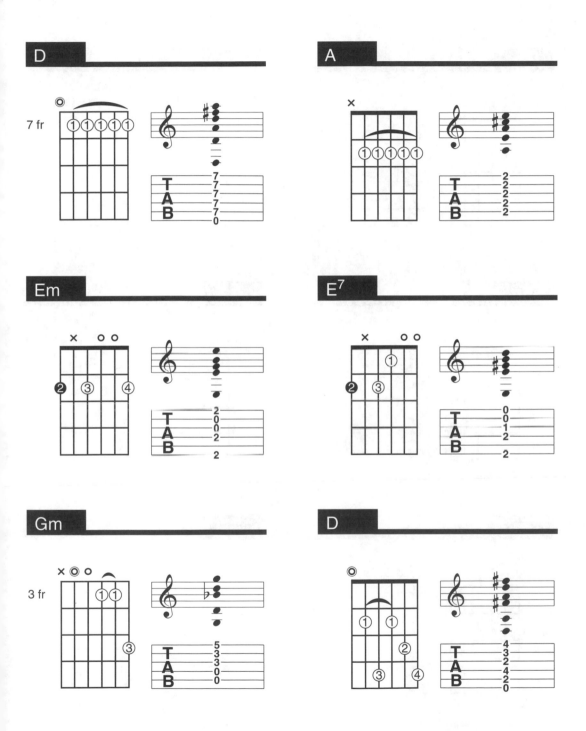

Once you've tried a few straight barre shapes (open G, C, D and A shown), try the more difficult seventh and minor examples here. I've also included the awkward but extremely useful 2nd fret version of D.

G chords

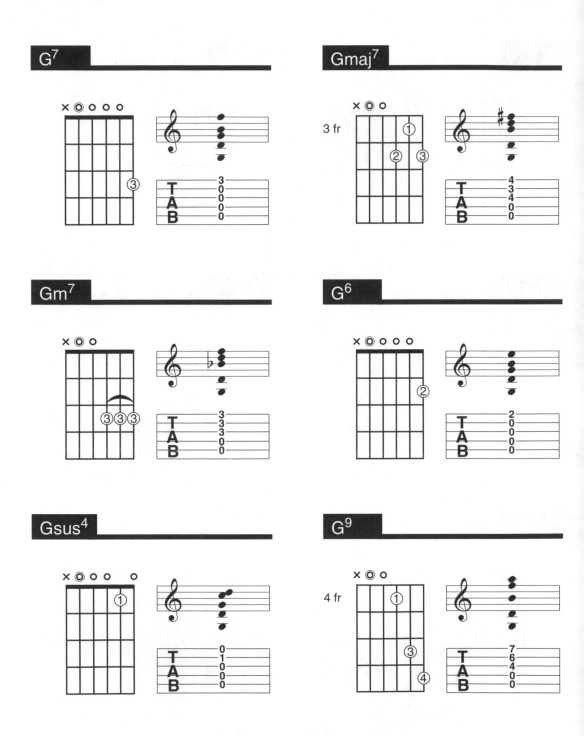

Because the tuning does so much of the work for you, most of the chords which have a root note of G are very easy to play. There are dozens more variations, many of which use only one finger.

Further ideas

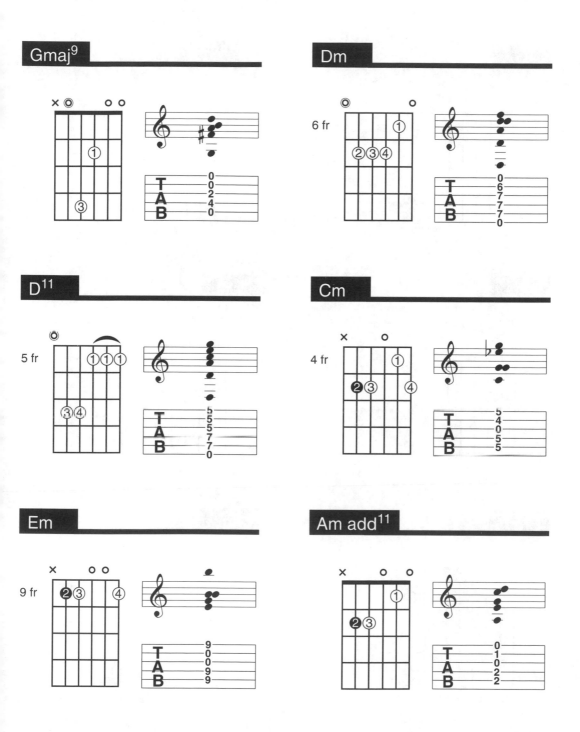

Gmaj⁹

Dm

D¹¹

Cm

Em

Am add¹¹

The price you have to pay for the convenience and sound of those G chords is that other shapes can be very difficult to work out. Here are some of the more unexpected shapes that the tuning allows.

Further ideas

Another use of altered bass notes is to create 'slash chords', where the chord and bass note are different. I've shown three examples, plus some other chords which you may find useful in the key of G.

'Woke Up This Mornin'

If you're new to bottleneck techniques, this simple blues riff is a great place to start. It demonstrates four slide techniques in the open G tuning – chord playing, double-stops, a single-note lick and vibrato. This type of lick is typical of Robert Johnson, and works equally well if, like him, you try it with a capo. Remember that the slide should be over, not between, the frets shown.

'Demerara Rock'

With the open 5th string acting as a drone note, you can alter the chords in rhythm to create some great riffs – Keith Richards has built a career on this idea! This example is typical of his style, and doesn't make any use of the two outer strings. Use up- and down-strokes, and don't worry too much about accuracy – it's fine if the open notes ring on a little longer than shown.

121

'Love Struck'

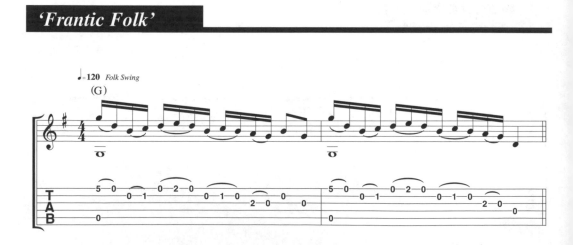

Once you've mastered the difficult D chord shape, the A and G chords here are a barre and an open chord respectively. You'll get the smoothest flow of notes if you use your thumb for the fifth and fourth strings, and three fingers for the first three strings. These techniques and shapes were used (with a capo) by Mark Knopfler in Dire Straits' *Romeo And Juliet.*

'Frantic Folk'

Once you start to let your playing work with the tuning, you'll find there are many technical advantages to playing in open G. This example features the ringing G bass note, while making maximum use of the hammer-ons and pull-offs available. If you can get your technique rhythmically accurate, you should be able to play this even faster than the ♩=120 shown.

Robert Johnson's classic blues recordings made use of open G and its variants.

6	5	4	3	2	1
D	A	D	F#	A	D
-2	0	0	-1	-2	-2

Open D is the deepest-sounding of the commonly-used open tunings. As a bottleneck tuning, it's the second most popular after open G. It's one of the few altered tunings to create a six-string major chord when strummed open, and this is perhaps why it has several variants – the two most common being open C (the whole tuning dropped a whole step) and open E (raised a whole step). Bear in mind that if you opt for open E, you'll have to raise the pitch of the fifth, fourth and third strings, increasing the risk of breakage. You might be better sticking with open D and using a 2nd fret capo if you want to play in the key of E.

Artists who have used the tuning include Joni Mitchell (who used it with a capo), Leo Kottke (who detuned it into lower registers), Eric Clapton and Pearl Jam.

Tuning Guide

Drop both the outer two strings down to D (see the first two chapters), then fret the fourth string at the fourth fret, creating a note of F#. Lower the pitch of the open third string until it matches exactly. Now play the (lowered) third string at the *3rd* fret, and lower the pitch of the second until it's the same. To check the second string, play it against a 12th fret harmonic of the 5th string – both should sound the same. Strum the full six-string open chord to check the D chord is in tune.

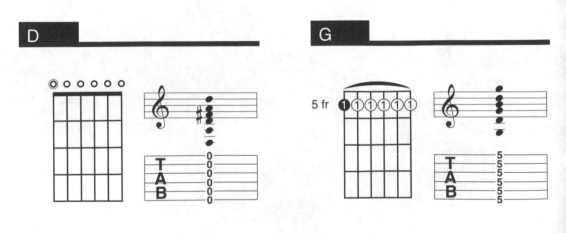

D   G

Basic chords

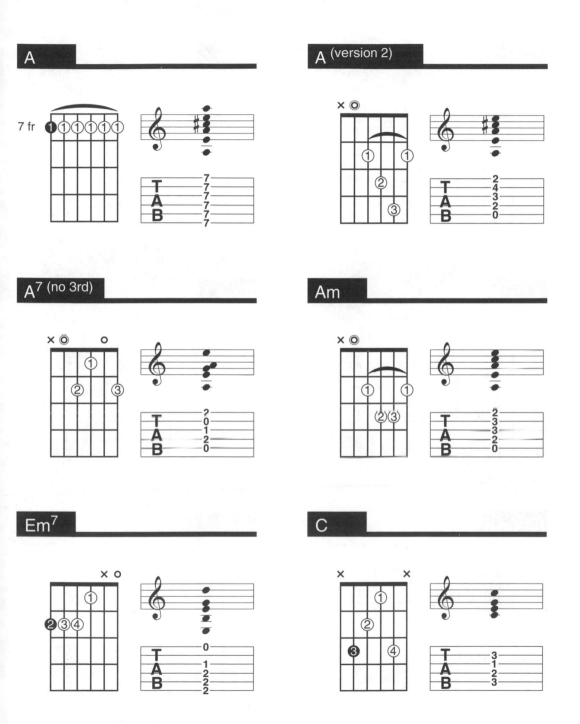

Due to the A bass note on the fifth string, chords with a root of A are as easy as some of the D chords available in this tuning. Some chords, like the Em7 and C shown here, require careful use of muting.

D chords

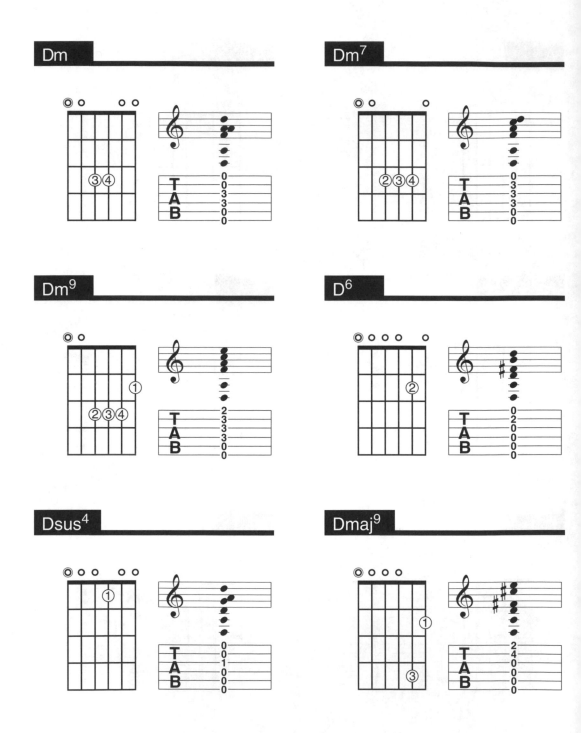

When your starting point is such a fantastic-sounding D chord, it doesn't take a lot of effort to come up with some good variations. Here are six of the simplest.

Further ideas

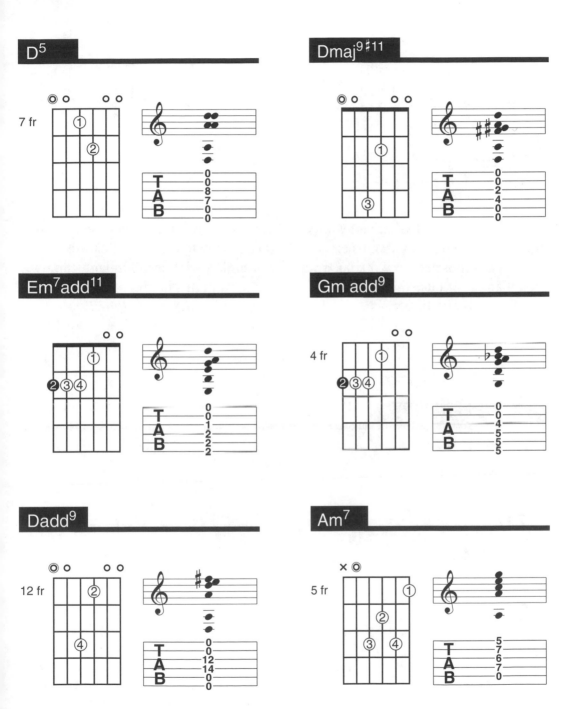

Despite the complex names, none of these chords is difficult. Two of these (Em7add11 and Gmadd9) use the common technique of moving a fretted shape around while keeping the first two strings open.

'Little Black Cab'

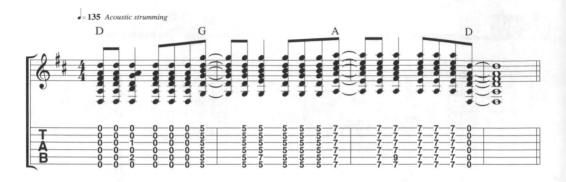

This acoustic rhythm part works equally well with or without a capo, and it's also possible to work out a version that doesn't use the open chord. It's based on one-finger six-string barre shapes, with extra fingers added and taken away to create new chords and rhythmic variations. Similar techniques are used in this tuning on Joni Mitchell's track *Big Yellow Taxi*.

'Delta Bad Card'

Open D tuning has also been used on early blues recordings by greats such as Son House, Elmore James and of course Robert Johnson. This descending outro line in the key of D is a typical example. Use all downstrokes with the plectrum, or play the double-stopped notes using two fingers at a time. Note the bluesy quarter-tone bend in the second bar.

Joni Mitchell never learned to play in normal tuning, but used over 50 of her own devising!

6	5	4	3	2	1
D	A	D	G	A	D
-2	0	0	0	-2	-2

The DADGAD tuning (pronounced 'Dad-Gad') is a curious beast – it sounds like it's been around for centuries, and is used to play many ancient folk tunes, and yet it was almost certainly invented by 1950s acoustic player Davey Graham. Since then, it's appeared on the acoustic recordings of Richard Thompson, Pierre Bensusan and Nick Harper, but never more famously than in the Led Zeppelin tracks *Black*

Mountain Side and *Kashmir*.

DADGAD, when strummed open, creates a chord of Dsus4. It isn't easy to get to grips with at first because it's not based on an open chord, and yet it is still altered very heavily from standard tuning, making new chord shapes difficult to play and to work out. However, once you've figured out even two or three basic shapes, the whole rune-clad Celtic world of magic and mystery is yours for the taking!

Tuning Guide

Starting from normal EADGBE tuning, drop the outer two strings to D as explained in previous chapters. Play the third string at the 2nd fret, then lower the tuning of the second string until the two are the same pitch. If your guitar has a particularly high action, you may find the harmonic method more accurate; play a 12th fret harmonic on the fifth string lower the 2nd string note until it matches. To check, fret the third string at the 2nd fret and strum all six.

Dsus⁴

D

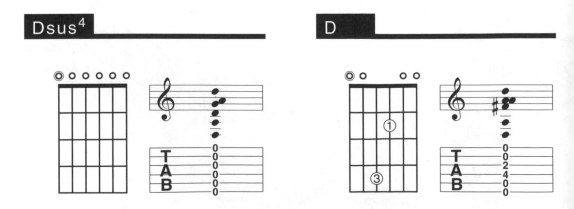

Basic chords

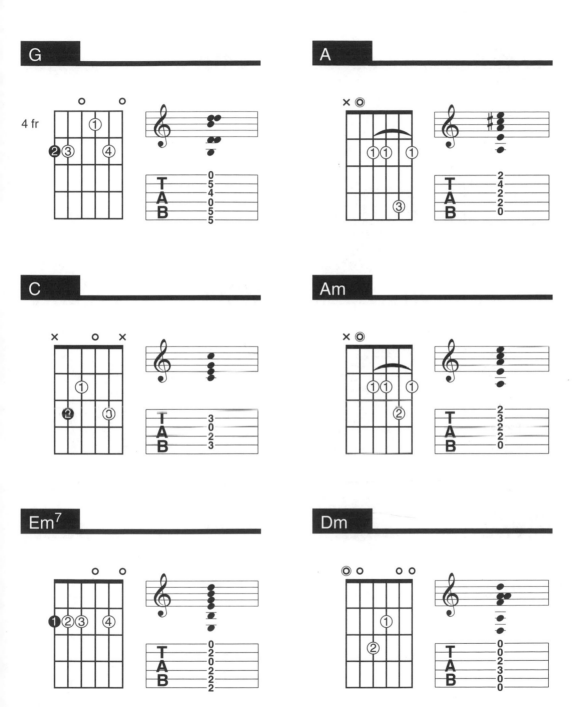

DADGAD isn't really designed for playing straight major and minor strummed chords, so don't worry if you find these chords more difficult than the ones with more obscure-sounding names.

D chords

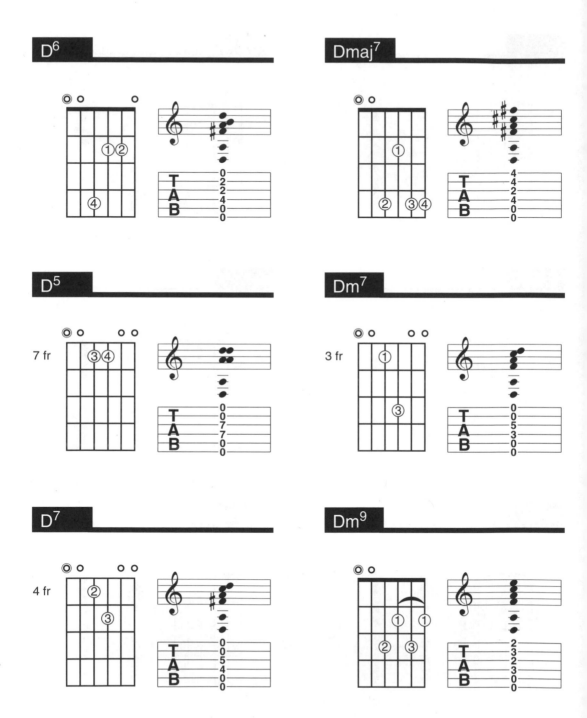

Despite the weird shapes, all of these chords are based in DADGAD's home key of D. Of these, the D5 is possibly the most useful because it has the open 'Gaelic' sound often associated with this tuning.

Further ideas

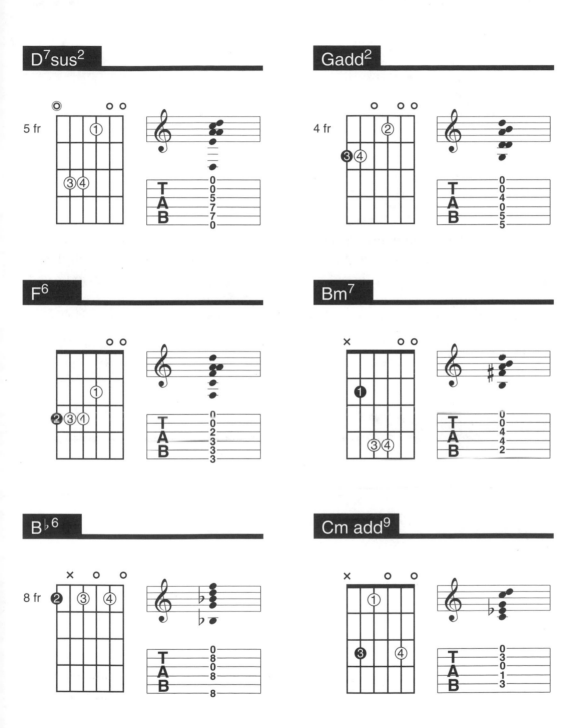

Note that because of the unusual tuning, some chords which you wouldn't normally associate with the key of D (e.g. Cmadd9, B♭6) fall fairly comfortably under the fingers.

'Maypole Dance'

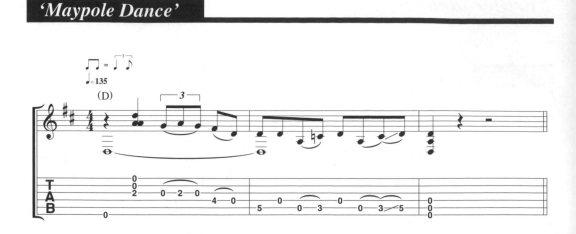

Folk guitarists often use the open strings associated with DADGAD for this type of Celtic effect. Although it's based on a drone-line chord of D5, the rapidly-shifiting melody implies chords of D7 and D. As with many folk-based styles, maximum use is made of the open strings as part of the melody, and hammer-ons and slides are used wherever possible.

'Wing And A Page'

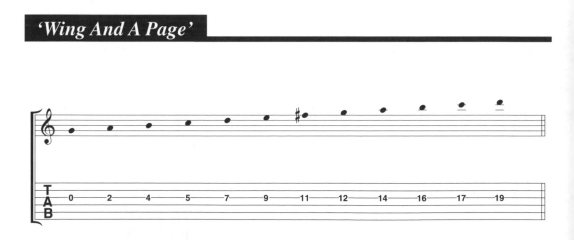

Here's a DADGAD trick that I've been using for years. Learn this scale (it's actually the D Mixolydian mode, theory fans) on the third string as shown, then slide your hand up and down the neck, choosing any notes of the scale that you think sound good. Now do the same thing while strumming all six strings. Hey presto – instant Led Zeppelin!

Folk player Richard Thompson went all Celtic with his DADGAD tuning.

There are no rules about what makes a good alternate tuning – if it works for you, then use it! Acoustic players of the '60s and '70s (notably Stephen Stills and Nick Drake) often made up tunings on the spot to suit their needs, and some more electrified artists such as Soundgarden and Sonic Youth have brought the 'devised' tuning right up to date.

In this chapter is a selection of some of the less common tunings, together with some ideas for adapting them to your own style and sound. All of these have been used on guitar recordings during the last 30 years, but they're not as accessible or immediate as some of the others we've looked at. Some of the examples (Nashville tuning particularly) will need different string gauges on your guitar. So if you break a string, don't send me the bill!

Open E5

6	5	4	3	2	1
E	B	E	E	B	E
0	+2	+2	-3	0	0

This tuning, and its semitone-dropped brother open E♭5, has been used by Stephen Stills and The Gary Glitter band. Although it creates a 'power chord' played open, its unison E notes can be very effective as part of an acoustic fingerstyle accompaniment.

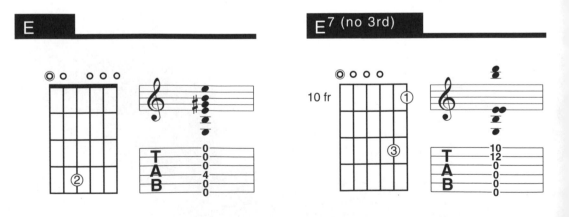

'Two Score And Nine'

In this fingerpicked example, the thumb plays the sixth and fourth strings only (both tuned to E), but the first finger covers the third string (also E), creating an interesting doubled note in the almost sitar-like accompaniment. The second and third fingers of the picking hand articulate the melody, which is played in intervals of thirds on the first two strings.

'#12 Chorus'

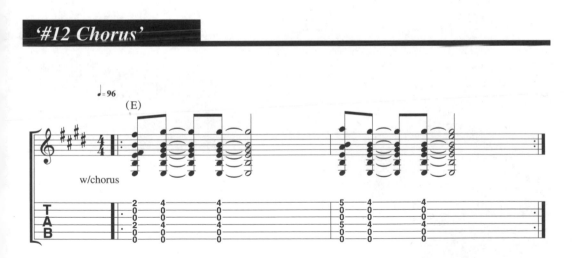

In this tuning, the in-built unisons and repeated octave notes imply a 12-string effect anyway, so it's a relatively simple matter to come up with finger shapes that make big, expansive acoustic chords. Both the fretted notes here are the same, albeit an octave apart. You might also like to try the same strings played up at the 7th, 9th, 10th, 11th and 12th frets.

This is one of the few photos of Nick Drake, who used open tunings extensively until his death at the age of 24.

Dropped Top D Tuning

6	5	4	3	2	1
E	A	D	G	B	D
0	0	0	0	0	-2

If you're only going to alter one string from regular tuning, it doesn't have to be in the bass end (for example, dropping the third string down to F♯) creates 'Lute' tuning, which many classical players still use).

This example simply lowers the first string by a tone – I call it 'lazy bottleneck' tuning because you can use it to play the majority of Open G slide lead licks (see page 23) without deviating too far from regular tuning when you're playing live. However, it also gives you the option of that ringing D note in any open chords you might come up with.

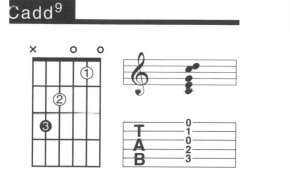

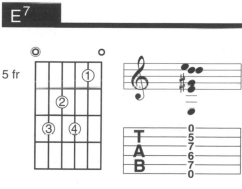

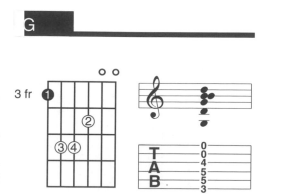

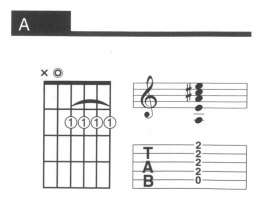

139

'All The Fourths' Tuning

6	5	4	3	2	1
E	A	D	G	C	F
0	0	0	0	+1	+1

Regular tuning is the most convenient and versatile compromise for the guitar (which is why we use it) but that doesn't necessarily make it the most logical. All orchestral stringed instruments (e.g. violin, 'cello, double bass) are tuned in fourths or fifths, rather than the combination of intervals that guitarists use.

'All The Fourths' uses the same interval between each string – so you put your finger on the fifth fret of *every* string when you're tuning the guitar to itself. It's not especially versatile, but many jazz players swear by it.

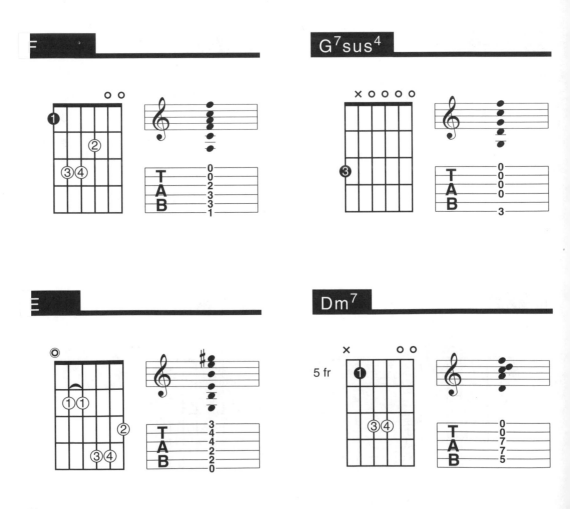

'New Clear Fusion'

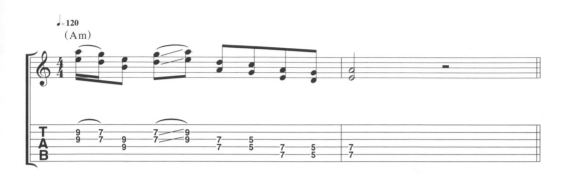

Although this type of parallel-4ths double-stopped riff is normally associated with jazz or fusion, the example shown here should word just as well in a rock format. The tuning allows you to play what would normally be a fairly difficult lick at greater speed due to the fact that all the double-stops can use the same flattened finger shape.

'Scale With Harmonics'

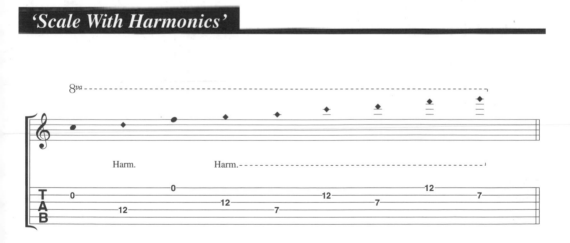

Every new tuning brings with it new opportunities for open harmonics, and this one is no exception. This is a scale of D minor pentatonic, played using a combination of open notes and open harmonics at the 12th and 7th frets. Play the scale as shown, then play it in reverse, making sure that all the open notes and harmonics ring on. The effect is very harp-like.

Nashville Tuning

6	5	4	3	2	1
E	A	D	G	B	E
+12	+12	+12	0	0	0

You can only really try this one out if you've got a spare guitar or a lot of patience, because it involves restringing every time you want to use it. Nashville tuning is identical to regular tuning except the three 'bass' strings are tuned an octave higher (suggested electric gauges .024-

.015-.012-.017-.013-.010). It creates a chiming, 'jangly' sound, and works equally well on electric and acoustic guitar. It's particularly easy to use because we already know all the chord shapes, but don't try to play straightforward solos unless you're prepared for some very strange results!

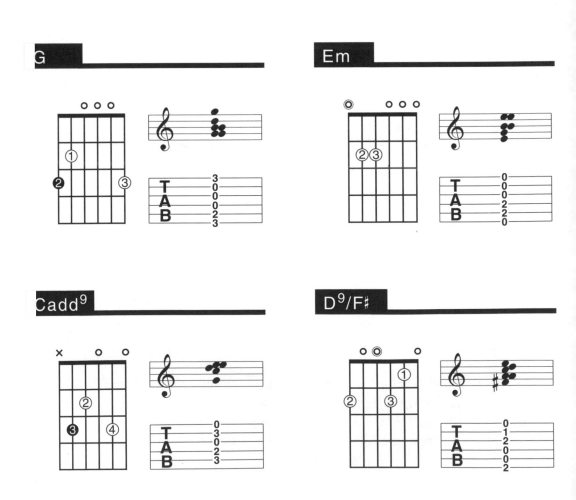

'Wrong Way Up'

This flash-sounding country picking lick is much simpler than it seems. Check out the tab and you'll see ordinary chord shapes of C, G and C again, played fingerstyle using three fingers and the thumb. However, because of all the confused octaves Nashville tuning gives us, the effect is quite startling. As long as you can play it as fast as those Nashville cats...

'Chiming Scale'

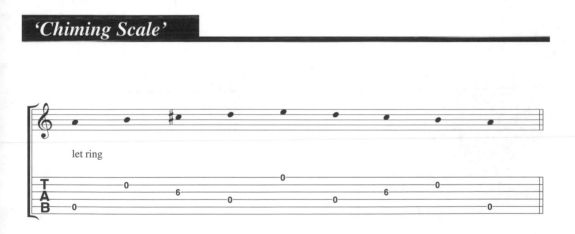

Nashville tuning has also recently been used by John Squire on Stone Roses' recordings, and this technique is a good example of the way electric players can use it in a more indie-rock context than its country name would suggest. Simply pick the strings shown while fretting the third string, and the resulting scale should give you loads of ideas for variations.

Jeff Buckley experimented with tunings in the 90s - just like his dad Tim in the 70s.

Hopefully the examples shown here should give you enough inspiration to devise some tunings of your own. Remember, there are no rules about what you can and can't do; as long as it sounds good, and your string gauge will cope with it, any tuning you devise is fair game. Listen to artists like Jeff Buckley and Bernard Butler to hear what can be achieved with imaginative use of tunings.

It's not worth spending a lot of time working out new fingerings for the familiar chords you normally use - you'll be wasting all of the creative potential of the tuning. Use altered tunings as they were meant to be used – to expand the range of sounds and textures you can produce from your guitar – and you'll be well on the way to becoming a better all-round musician.

Do...

- ...figure out whether your string gauge can cope with the tuning. If you're playing electric guitar fitted with .009 gauge strings, you won't get a particularly great sound out of Open C tuning, for example, unless you select a higher gauge.

- ...devise your own tunings. Try starting with one from this book, then altering one note to see what results it produces – e.g. if you start in Open D tuning and drop the third string down a half step (semitone) you get open D minor.

- ...make sure you're exactly *in tune*. Often a tuing might sound terrible simply because the notes aren't completely accurate. Check and double check, using a tuner if you have one.

- ...try using fingerstyle. By far the most frequent users of altered tunings are acoustic players, so if you've used a plectrum all your life, now's a great time to become a picker!

- ...try using bottleneck. You'll probably find that the open chord tunings work better for straight blues chords licks, but all of the tunings in the book have the *potential* for slide.

- ...experiment with capos. If you put the guitar in open D tuning, put a capo at the 4th fret and you've got instant open F# tuning.

- ...drop me a cyber-line! joe.bennett@ndirect.co.uk

Don't...

- ...tune up too far! If you're raising any note by more than a whole step (two frets' worth) you're substantially increasing the risk of string breakage. If in doubt, figure out the whole tuning a step lower, and use a capo.

- ...be put off if the tuning doesn't sound good when all the notes are played open. Not all 'altered' tunings have to create a chord on their own. Maybe you just have to find the right fingering to get the best out of it.

- ...rely too much on your usual techniques. For example, if bends work well on the third string in regular tuning, perhaps the altered version might be more flattering to another string?

- ...strum every chord you see in this book. Some of the chord shapes work better played fingerstyle, and some may be more effective when picked one note at a time.

- ...give up too soon on a tuning. It might have taken many years to get to your current level in regular tuning, so be prepared to put in the hours before you hear something really good.

- ...try all the examples in the book on the same instrument. Some of them work better on acoustic, some on electric, some both.

- ...forget which tuning you're using half-way through a song. Very embarrassing indeed!

About Guitar Riffs And Licks

As practising guitarists, we spend hour after hour learning new scales and chords in the hope that it will make us into better players. Then, as soon as we play a gig or jam with other musicians, all the learning can go out of the window, and we end up playing the riffs and licks we know and love so well. Why?… because they sound good! Riffs are an essential part of every guitar player's vocabulary – ignore them at your peril.

This book includes many 'classic' phrases that guitar players have been using for decades. You'll hear these, and variations on them, in thousands of recordings across a range of styles.

One thing that you'll notice about many of the riffs here is that they're fairly simple. Riffing's not the same as soloing – you're not out to wow an audience with your technique, just engage their ears.

Most great guitar players have an armoury of riffs and licks which they use so often that they become part of their individual style. We've all been stealing shamelessly from each other for years, so there's nothing wrong with using the ideas from this book to invent your own killer riff, then writing a million-selling guitar classic!

What's a riff?

- A riff is a repeating phrase which forms a 'hook' for the listener. It can appear in intros and outros, though sometimes riffs are played between parts of a song, or even throughout verses and choruses.

- Riffs are usually one, two or four bars in length.

- Often, simple riffs are the most effective, because they're more memorable.

- Most riffs are played in the lower register of the guitar, rather than way up the neck.

- Classic rock intro riffs include – Deep Purple's *Smoke On The Water*, Led Zeppelin's *Whole Lotta Love*, Free's *All Right Now*, Aerosmith's *Walk This Way* and The Beatles' *I Feel Fine*.

What's a lick?

- A lick is a learned melodic line which a guitarist will use during a solo or lead part. It generally only appears once or twice in a piece of music, and doesn't form the central 'hook'.

- Licks can be any length, but are usually one bar or less.

- Licks can be as ridiculously flash as you like. That's why they're worth learning!

- Licks can be played anywhere on the guitar fingerboard.

- Some people use the term 'riff' when they mean 'lick'. Really, the only difference is that riffs are played over and over. So it's fair to say that all riffs are licks, but not all licks are riffs!

Even if you learn the riffs and licks in this book as 'shapes' rather than as collections of notes, it's always handy to have an idea of the actual notes you're playing. Below are two complete fret diagrams showing all of the note names for the first 12 frets of the guitar, in both flats and sharps versions. If you keep the note names in mind when you learn a new riff, your fretboard knowledge will quickly improve.

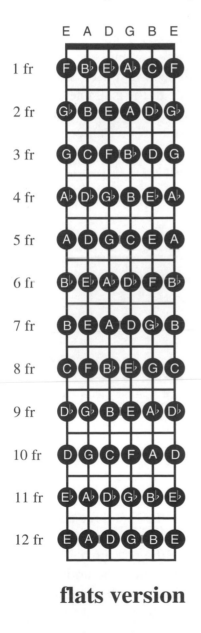

flats version

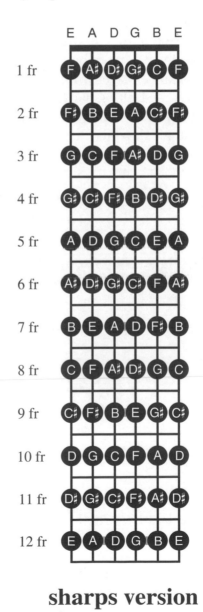

sharps version

149

In this first chapter, all the riffs have one thing in common – they're dead easy! This is not to say they sound better or worse than any of the other examples in the book – remember, a difficult riff is not necessarily a great one. These five riffs all make use of open strings (for more on this, see page 28) and can be played with one or two fingers of the fretting hand.

Even if you're a fairly experienced player, don't skip this chapter! These riffs and their musical cousins have created the backing for some of the most famous rock and blues guitar tracks of all time.

When you're trying out a riff, start slowly and build up to speed. Make sure each note rings clearly, with no hint of fret buzz. Note that four of these five examples should be repeated, so keep practising until each riff can be 'looped' back into itself smoothly.

As with all the examples, suggested metronome speeds are included for practice purposes, but feel free to play each new riff at whatever speed you think sounds good.

'Lookin' For Trouble?'

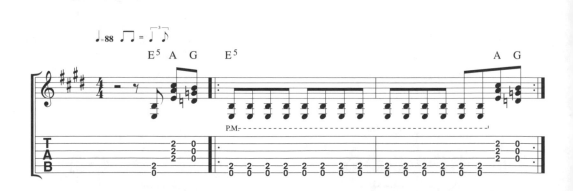

This laid-back rhythm part can be traced back to blues greats such as Robert Johnson and Blind Lemon Jefferson, but it has also been used by Elvis Presley and even AC/DC.

After the first three chords, only play the two bass strings, resting the palm of the picking hand gently on the strings near the bridge as you play to create a 'palm mute'.

'Purple Rock'

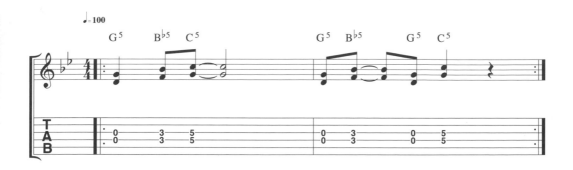

This powerful riff sounds great with distortion, and can be be played with one finger (although you'll get a smoother effect if you use your first and third fingers to fret notes).

Because the fretted notes are played on the middle two strings of the instrument, you should take care to avoid open strings sounding, especially if you're using distortion.

'Shake A Wish'

This two-bar repeating phrase could be used as an accompaniment to a verse, or as a solo riff on its own. It's especially effective when played in unison with a bass.

Play each note with a downstroke, and fret each note cleanly – there should be no additional note created when you take a finger off a string.

'Blues Downer'

This is more of a lick than a riff, because it would just sound too repetitive if it were played over and over. Still, it's a great way to start or end a simple blues solo.

The 'double-stops' at the start should sound at exactly the same time as each other. Use the third finger to play notes at the third fret, and the second finger for notes at the second.

'Parfitt Day'

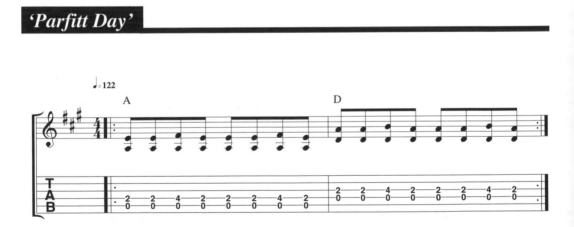

This driving rock-style accompaniment is actually a variation on the blues riff shown on page 6 – it's just played with a 'straight' rather than 'swing' rhythm.

Here, each bar features the riff played over a different chord, so you'll need to move smoothly between pairs of strings at the end of each bar.

Deep Purple's Ritchie Blackmore, burning up the fretboard with some of the 1970s' hottest riffs.

There's often more to chord playing than simple song accompaniment. Sometimes, the chords themselves can form a riff. Think of Nirvana's *Smells Like Teen Spirit*, The Who's *Pinball Wizard*, Eddie Cochran's *Summertime Blues*, or The Manic Street Preachers' *Kevin Carter*. Chord riffs, every one.

Usually a chordal riff involves some sort of movement between chords, but rarely a complex one. Just the action of strumming some repeated changes can cement the riff into the listener's head –

for example, the classic opening sequence from the Motown hit *Knock On Wood* uses a single open E barre chord shape moved to the third, fifth, seventh and tenth fret positions and back again over four bars.

All of the examples in this chapter use the chords in a particular rhythmic way. So when you're trying to come up with your own ideas, remember that a good chordal riff uses a combination of chord changes and rhythm ideas – it's not always enough simply to strum the chords randomly.

'White On Black'

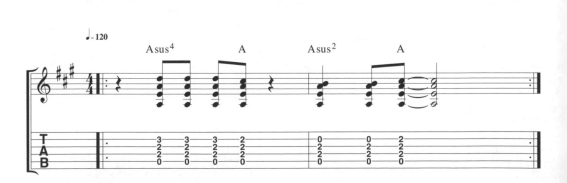

This rhythmic two-bar riff is loosely based on Slash's riff from Michael Jackson's single *Black And White*. It works particularly well with a 'crunch' overdrive.

Even though the riff is instantly memorable, it just consists of simple variations around an open A chord, created by changing the notes on the second string.

'Smells Like A Chord Riff'

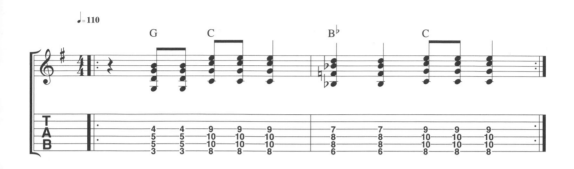

The idea of using two chord changes in a two-bar riff is typically Nirvana, but you can also hear these ideas in riffs by The Kinks, AC/DC and Oasis.

Although these chords can be played in various different positions, they are shown here as a single moveable barre chord shape to demonstrate the simplicity of the riff.

'Wild Chords'

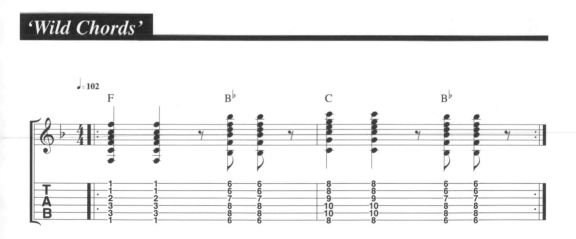

Here, the chords are so simple that they need this strong rhythmic hook to make them effective as a riff. You can hear this type of change in songs such as *Wild Thing* and *You've Lost*

That Lovin' Feeling.
Full barre chords are shown here, but you could just as easily strum only a few notes from each chord.

'God's Chord Tree'

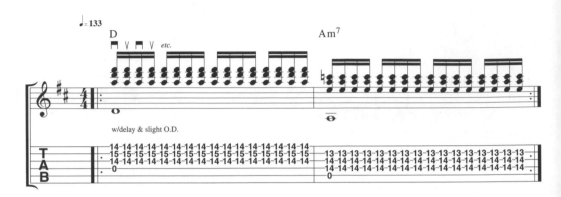

This U2-style riff uses rapid rhythmic up- and down-strokes, while the open string rings on under the chord. The chord change to Am7 is fairly difficult at this speed, so practise the changes slowly to begin with.

Use the little finger of your fretting hand to stop any unwanted open strings from sounding.

'Current Chords'

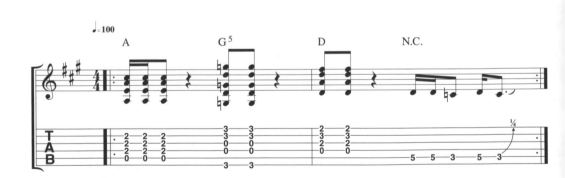

You can thank AC/DC's Angus for this killer three-chord riff. The band have built a reputation on solid, laser-accurate rhythm guitar phrases like this one.

Use a moderate distortion sound, and make sure you mute any notes which aren't currently being played with the remaining fingers of your fretting hand.

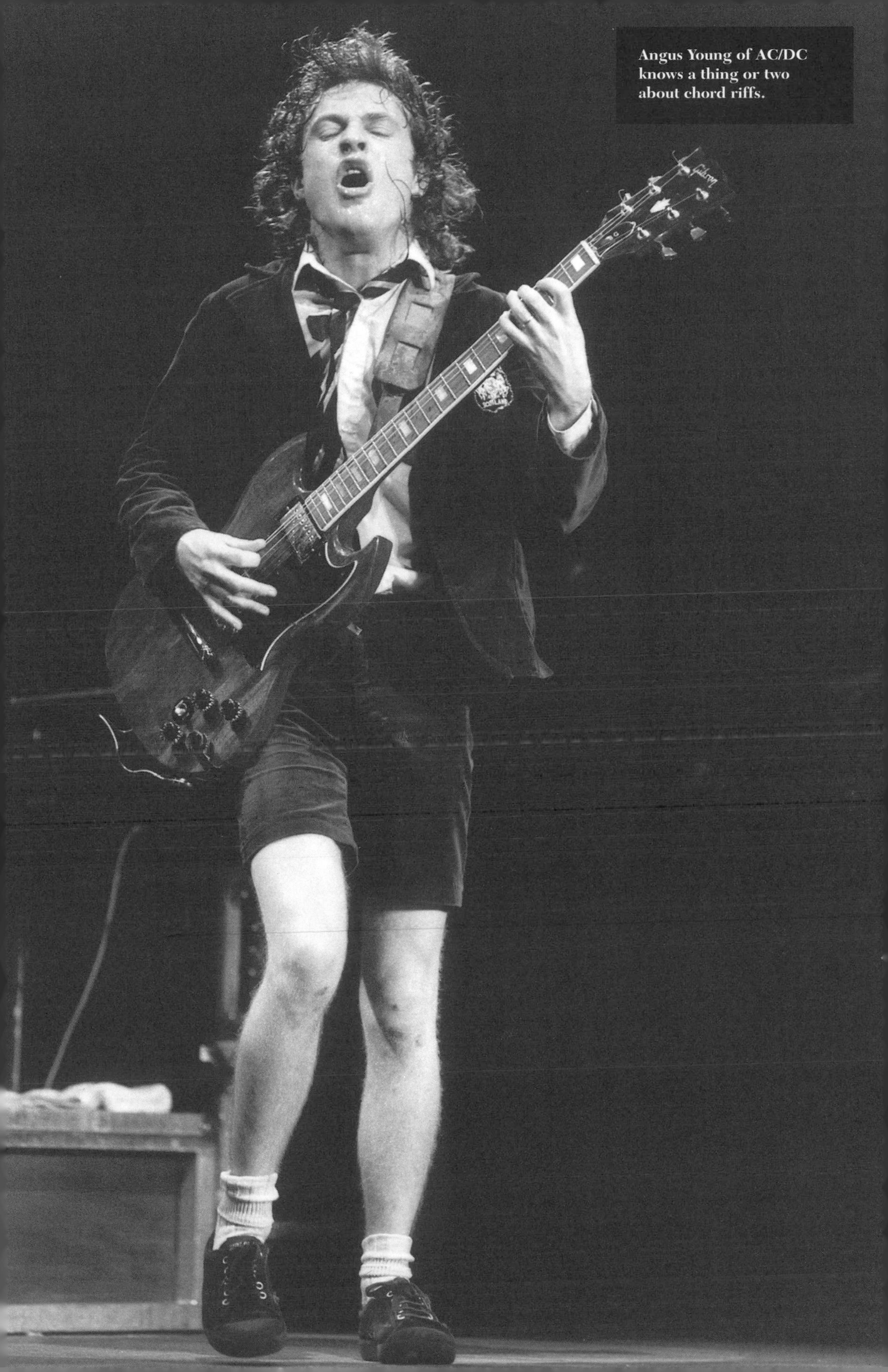

Angus Young of AC/DC knows a thing or two about chord riffs.

D ouble-stops are simply two notes played together. Although you *can* play double stops fingerstyle, they're more commonly played with a plectrum – usually using downstrokes.

The technique is not particularly new – early blues players often played two notes at once to thicken solo parts, and some jazz players of the 40s and 50s used double-stopped licks to create complex harmonised lead lines. But in terms of rock music, the pioneer of the technique was, without a doubt, Chuck Berry (see page 18). His solos were

entirely built up of learned licks, but strung together in such a way that his style was instantly recognisable.

Other exponents of the double-stopped lick include; Marc Bolan, ZZ Top, U2 and Led Zeppelin (see examples), plus contemporary bands such as Ocean Colour Scene, Blur and Green Day.

To play a double-stop, make sure that you catch both notes together – they should sound as one note rather than two strings played one after the other. Use positive downstrokes with the plectrum, but don't grip it too tightly.

'Mini Driver'

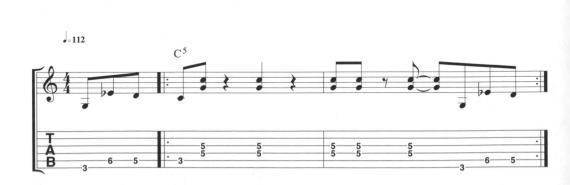

This syncopated double-stopped lick is based on some of the simple rock accompaniments played by Marc Bolan and T. Rex in the early 1970s.

It's particularly versatile as it works equally well with or without distortion. Lift your fingers slightly from the fretboard after each double-stop to cut some notes short.

'Brown-Eyed Van'

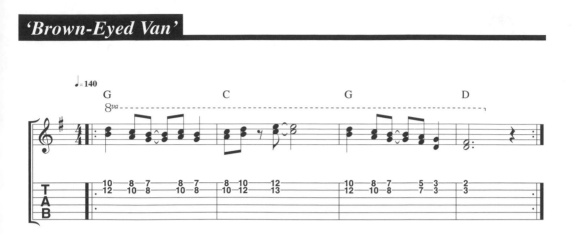

One well-loved use of the double-stopping is to harmonise lead lines. It can be tricky to do because you have to work out in advance which harmonies work and which don't, but the rewards are well worth it.

You might have difficulty shifting position at first – practise moving between the two shapes before you attempt the whole riff, being careful not to catch any of the lower strings.

'Minor Incident'

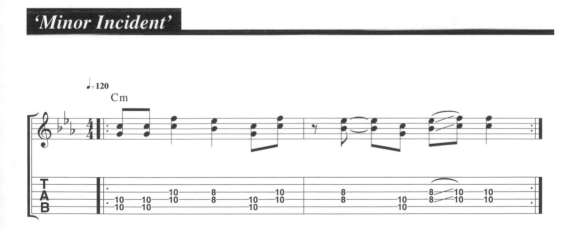

These rock-styled double-stops should be played with one finger flattened over two strings – try using your first finger for the notes at the 8th fret, and the third for those at the

10th. When you play the sliding note in bar 2, slide the first finger up while still fretting the chord, moving back into position in time for the repeat of the first bar.

159

'Blues Boogie'

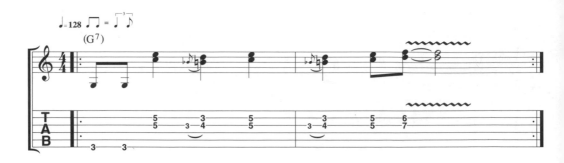

This subtle blues vamp sounds equally effective, whether you play it on its own as an intro, quietly under a bluesy vocal, or right up front as a solo line!

Because all the notes are fretted, you can move the whole shape up to the 8th fret to create a C7 riff, or the 10th fret to create a D7 riff.

'Water Works'

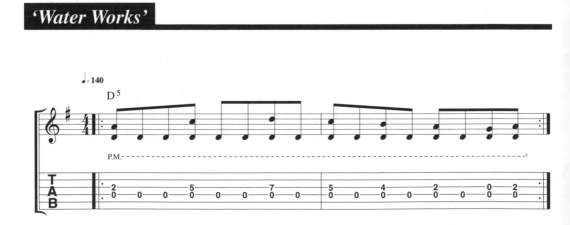

The idea of playing an open string and sliding a note around on an adjacent string has been well-used by indie and alternative guitarists since the 1970s. This version is in the key of D, and should be played with downstrokes throughout. Compression, delay and chorus effects could work here, but go easy on the distortion.

'Driving Along'

Although many players would suggest that this lick is vintage Chuck Berry, it's actually much older – the inspiration for this one actually comes from blues great Robert Johnson.

Experiment with different combinations of down- and up-strokes until the first six double-stops flow evenly.

'Classic Turnaround'

Although not strictly a double-stop (i.e. the notes aren't exactly played together) the techniques in this blues lick are so useful that they had to be included here.

Use two fingers (or pick and one finger) to pick notes on the third and first strings respectively as you slide the two-finger shape down the neck in the first bar.

'Berry Solo'

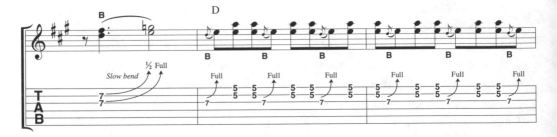

Because Chuck Berry's solos are so important in terms of the development of licks and riffs, I've included a full 12-bar blues sequence using some of his favourite musical phrases. Use downstrokes for every one of the double-stops.

Chuck Berry –
pioneer of the
double-stopped solo.

4

Bass-Note Riffs

All of the riffs in this section use the lower register of the guitar. A common misconception about all 'lead' playing is that it has to be high up the neck, and the examples shown here demonstrate that there are cool sounds to be had out of the bass strings too.

Bass-note riffs are particularly effective when played together with – you guessed it – a bass player! As with all riffs in the lower register of the guitar, you should avoid accidentally sounding any higher-pitched open strings as you play. Many players find it helpful to rest any 'unused' fingers of the fretting hand on unwanted strings for this reason.

'Deep Night'

This rock boogie example sounds best when played at full tilt with an angry drummer and a 100W Marshall stack!

Bars 3 and 4 of the riff suggest a rock accompaniment style, leaving a brief pause before the repeated riff thunders in again. Palm-mutes (see page 6) could be used on the open E bass string at this point.

'Dark Sunday'

This Black-Sabbath-meets-Metallica riff is our first example in an altered tuning. In this case, we're using 'dropped D' (the bass E string is detuned a whole tone to D).

This means you can play moving power chords with only one finger. Pile on the distortion, and release the palm mute where indicated to create dramatic accents.

'Comet Rock'

Here, the plectrum picks higher fretted notes inbetween notes of the basic bass note riff to create a rhythmic shuffle effect. You can play this as a one-bar riff (just keep repeating the first bar) or as a two-bar accompaniment (keep repeating bars 2 and 3).

'Useless Information'

Nothing could be simpler than this single-note two-bar phrase, but stomp on a fuzz pedal and play it in front of a pumping '60s R&B backing band, and you'll soon hear why it works so well.

You can play this example with up- or down-strokes as you wish, but down-strokes only will generally give a more driving, aggressive feel.

'New Jersey Dock'

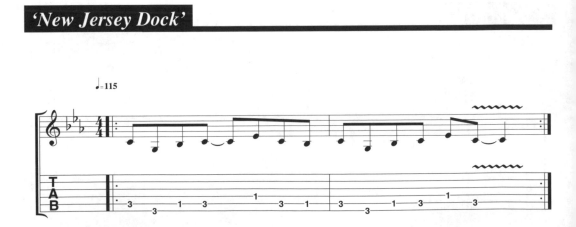

This Bon Jovi-influenced riff is one of many in this book to be based on the minor pentatonic scale. Although it looks quite 'busy', if you look carefully you'll notice there are only four notes in the whole riff.

Ideally, you should play this example with downstrokes, with a distortion or heavy overdrive effect.

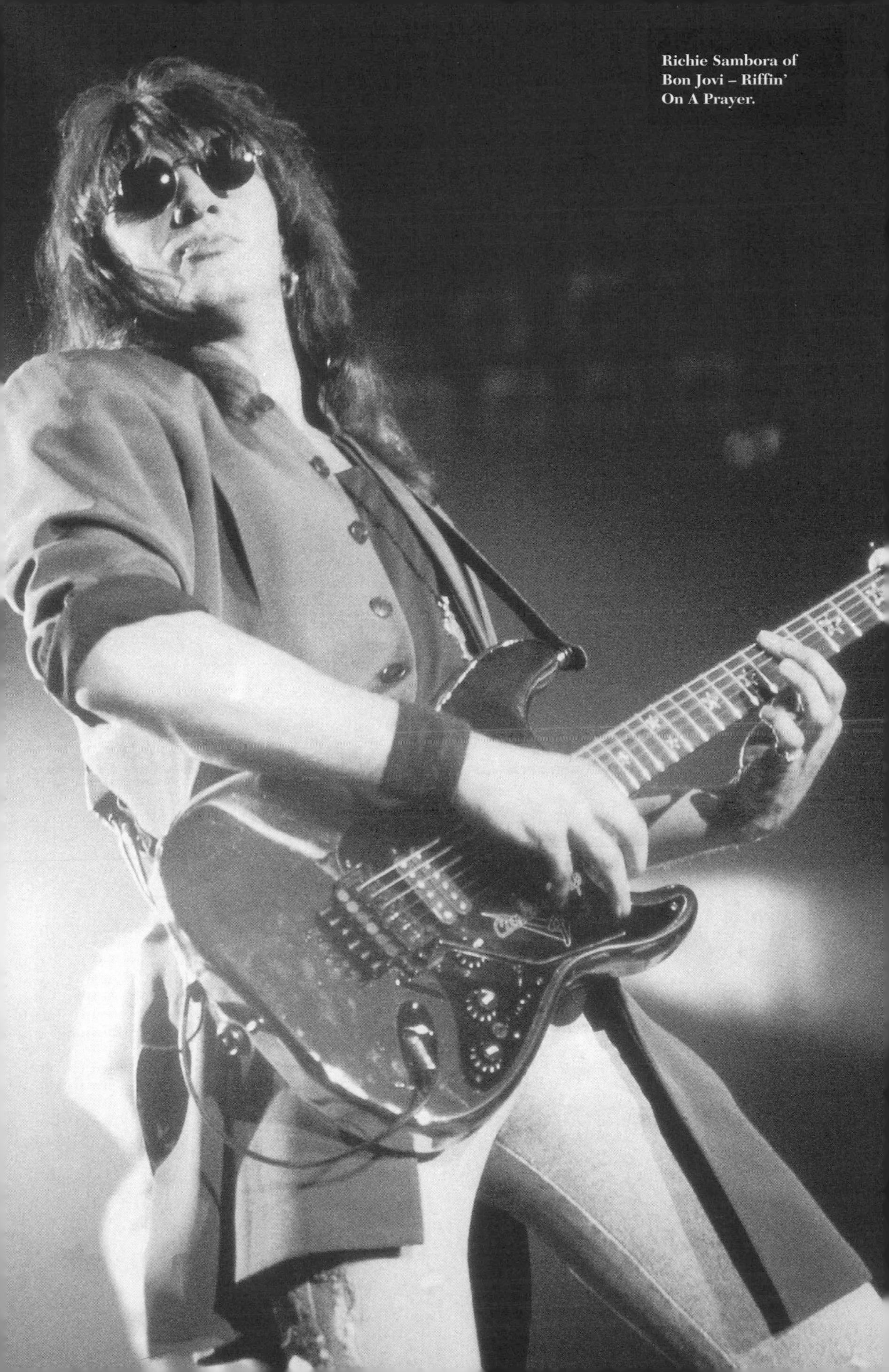

Richie Sambora of Bon Jovi – Riffin' On A Prayer.

5

Riffs And Licks With Bends

Ask any rock or blues guitarist to 'take a solo' and 99 times out of 100 they'll use bends. Perhaps surprisingly though, few of the great *riffs* of all time have actually used string-bending. However, plenty of the *licks* feature bends galore. Ever been stuck for what to play when you're in the middle of a solo? Pick a note, bend it up and hold it there. If you also manage to adopt a tortured facial expression the audience will come away thinking you played the whole solo with 'loads of feel'. Sounds dishonest? Hey, it works for me!

The licks in this section are designed to give you some ideas beyond the soloing cliché I've just described. Most of them use bends in conjunction with other ideas (e.g. held notes or cross-picking) to create licks that can enhance a solo if used in the right way.

Electric guitarists who have made bends a part of their style are too numerous to list here, but here are a few of the most famous; Eric Clapton, George Harrison, Noel Gallagher, Jimi Hendrix, Paul Weller, Carlos Santana. Still not convinced? You must be a jazz player...

'Bend And Hold'

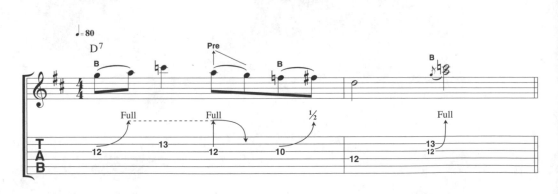

Bending one note while holding another isn't easier, but it creates such a beautiful country-blues sound if you get it right that it's definitely worth attempting.

For this example, I'd suggest you use the third finger to play all of the bends, and the little finger to hold the note on the second string. Let all notes ring on as long as possible.

'Two-Way Traffic'

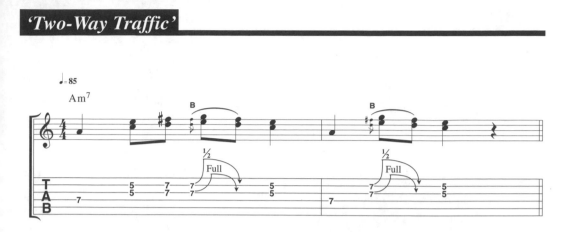

One strange thing about bends is that if you play them as a double-stop, the strings are bent up by different pitches. This is due to a combination of technique, finger strength and string gauge, but it's something we can make use of.

Bend using the little finger on the second string and the third on the third string.

'Cross Picked Bend'

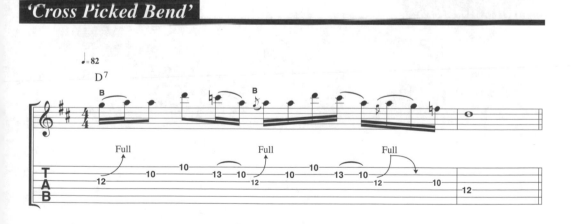

Played slowly, this lick creates a relaxed, country feel, but if you can manage it at full-on rock speed, it turns into something Gary Moore would be proud of!

Play the bend using your third finger, but keep the first finger flattened across the first two strings at the 10th fret. You'll be surprised at how fast you can play it with practice.

'White Witch'

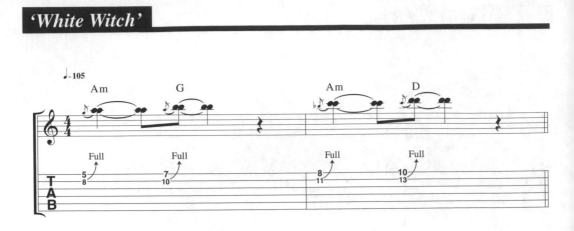

If you bend one note up so that it matches the pitch of the note on the next string, then hit both as a double-stop, you'll hear this distinctive 'screeching' noise, which sounds even better if you add distortion.

Carlos Santana made this lick part of his style in the early 1970s, and has continued to use it ever since.

'Numb Fingers'

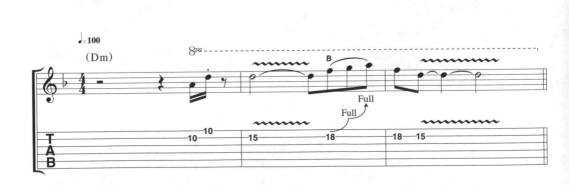

You'll need strong fingers for this one, because it's based on the movements of one David Gilmour's muscular digits. Many Pink Floyd solos include the technique of bending a note up a whole tone, then bending it a further whole tone (a total of four frets' worth!). This takes strength and patience (not to mention pain) but it sounds amazing.

BB King – master
of the bluesy
bending lick.

6

Riffs Using Open Strings

When most of us first learn guitar, the first chords we come across use open shapes – mainly because they're easier. Then we discover moveable barre chords, and for a while leave the open chords behind. It takes an imaginative player to make creative use of open strings, and this is even more apparent when trying to incorporate them into riffs.

These examples all use at least one open string, but are considerably more difficult than the beginners' open shapes shown on page 6.

Even though open string riffs are difficult to transpose to new keys, and may not always be able to use vibrato, they do have some advantages. Firstly, the open notes will have a different tone from the fretted ones. Secondly, it's often easier to play a riff with open strings because the finger-stretches are not as great. Thirdly, leaving open strings ringing while you move fretted shapes round the neck can give you new ideas which might not have occurred to you if you were using normal chord and scale shapes.

'Blue Lightning'

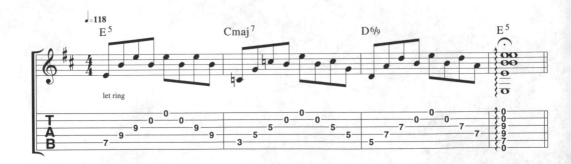

Suzanne Vega, Ozzy Osborne and The Manic Street Preachers have all had a hand in the shapes behind this sliding open-string riff.

The idea here is to play a fretted

chord shape (in this case, an E5) and move it around the neck while leaving the first two strings open. Try different chords and rhythms in order to make up your own riffs.

'Open Waterfall'

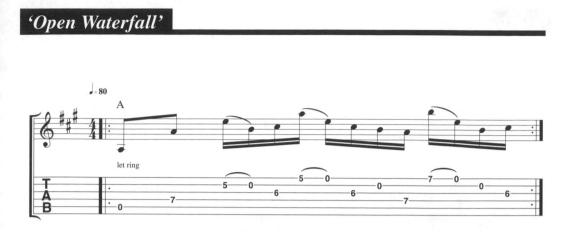

The combination of low and high open strings, fretted notes half-way up the neck, hammer-ons and fingerpicking creates a cascading 'waterfall' of notes.

This example shows the shape at the 5th fret, but you could also move it 2 frets lower, while maintaining the same open strings – the effect is reminiscent of a 12-string guitar.

'Keef's Chords'

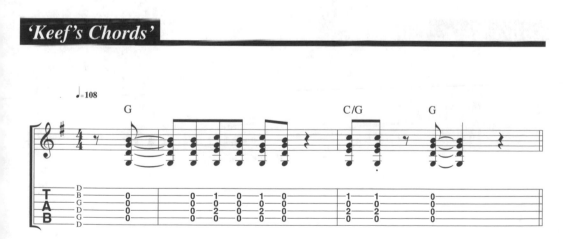

One of the world's most famous exponents of the chordal riff is the Rolling Stones' Keith Richards. He plays a five-string Fender Telecaster most of the time, but you can get close to the sound of his riffs by using the open G tuning shown here.

This two-chord example works equally well as an intro, verse accompaniment or outro.

'Desireability'

Here, the fretting hand slides up until the fretted note is the same pitch as the adjacent open note – it's a sliding version of *White Witch* on page 26.

You can use this technique with any of the open strings, though it's usually most effective on the first three. This example is based on Edge's techniques in U2's *Desire*.

'Triple Blue'

Another handy thing to remember about open notes is that you don't need to think about fretting them, so the fingers can be otherwise employed making your licks flow

more smoothly. In the case of this descending bluesy run of triplets, single or double pull-offs are used to add speed and fluidity to the lick.

'Tied Down'

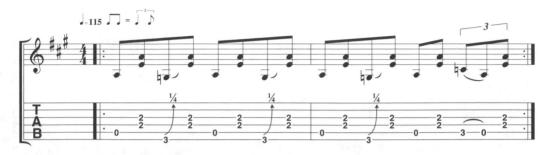

Use your flattened first finger to fret the double-stopped chord at the second fret. Reach over with your second or third finger to play the third fret notes on the bottom two strings.

'Rollin' Bunker'

Here is an example of how a fingerstyle player might approach a simple chord sequence like this.

Note the hammer-ons, which are picked with the thumb.

'Sheryl's In G'

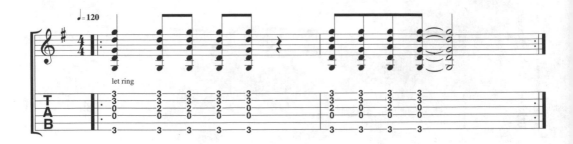

Sometimes, all a good chord riff needs is a carefully placed finger here and there.

This LA-style Sheryl Crow phrase uses a simple G chord with the 5th string muted.

'Ominous Intro'

You know that bit in the intro to metal songs before the band crashes in?

They're often riffs like this – again, the fretted notes move while the open ones stay the same.

Ozzy Osborne, with
metal intro supremo,
the late Randy Rhoads.

If you've read another of the books in this series (*Guitar Chords To Go!*) you'll know that power chords can be a guitarist's best friend when you're putting together a rhythm part. But there's no reason you can't use them to make up rock riffs as well.

In this section, all of the fretted riffs use a single power chord shape, moved to different positions on the neck. There's also an example of a riff using open power chords (see *'Who's There'* on page 36). Any riff or backing part which uses power chords will sound OK with distortion or overdrive, which is one reason why this type of riff is so often used in rock and metal. With these examples, it's even more important to mute unwanted open strings with your fretting hand fingers, because these additional notes will interfere with the sound, especially if you're using lots of distorted gain.

Famous power chord riffers include; Tony Iommi (*Black Sabbath*), Pete Townshend (*The Who*), Dave Grohl (*Foo Fighters*), Ace (*Skunk Anansie*) and Joe Perry (*Aerosmith*).

'Cross Inversion'

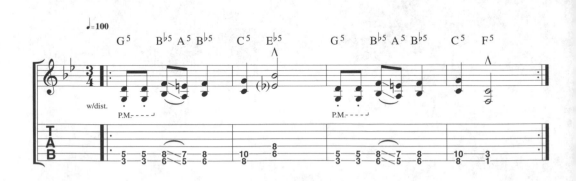

This riff uses a combination of palm-mutes, slides, and accents to create a typically metal-style bridge section. Note the unusual timing – count three to the bar throughout.

Use downstrokes with the plectrum for all the chords, but don't re-pick the chord when you slide down one fret to the A5 – hold the chord as you slide and it will still sound.

Metallica riff-meister James Hetfield helps supply the driving sound of the band's doubled power chord riffs.

'Metal Sunshine'

Sometimes, the rests between chords are as important as the chords themselves. This example uses power chords played after the beats of the bar in order to build tension and add rhythmic excitement.

The D5 to E5 change could be played as a sliding chord if you prefer.

'Who's There?'

Pete Townshend was such an influence on the way guitarists play power chords that an element of his style has to be included here. This example uses his trademark rapid up/downstroke before a long, ringing power chord. Note that the G5 chord has the fifth string muted – try to do this with the side of the second finger as you fret the bass note.

'Proud Of U'

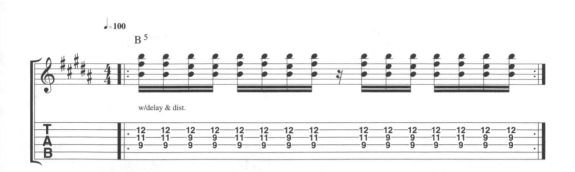

Even though this riff contains some rapid changes (created by adding and removing the third finger from a basic shape), both of the sounds created are actually power chords – they're just unusual shapes.

Try using a fast up-and-down strumming motion with your picking hand, making sure you only hit these three strings.

'Sliding Sevens'

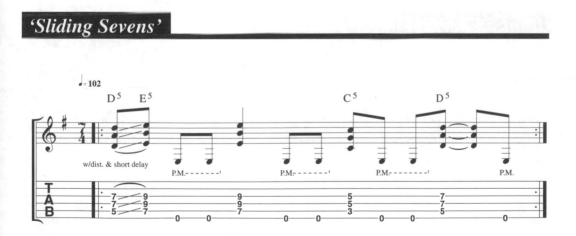

For the last 30 years, rock and metal bands experimented with unusual rhythms and weird time signatures. This one's in 7/4, and it's a kind of Black Sabbath meets The Chili Peppers hybrid!

Note how the palm mutes are applied on the bass notes only – this creates accents, throwing the rhythm out still further.

181

However much we all want to be serious musicians, there's a time when every guitarist wants to show off. But we don't necessarily want to put years of work into superfast alternate picking licks just so we can impress our friends.

This chapter features some *fairly* easy riffs and licks which sound more difficult than they actually are. Most of them use 'legato' techniques (i.e. tapping, hammer-ons and pull-offs) to aid speed. However, these examples are not purely for the sake of your ego – they're all perfectly useable in solos, if you can do so without stepping beyond the boundaries of good taste!

A brief word on technique; when you're using right-hand tapping, you'll probably get a lot of additional noise from the open strings. Some players use specially-made string mutes to stop this from happening, but there are plenty of ways you can learn to use the edge of the tapping hand or parts of the fretting hand to maintain the mutes.

These techniques appear in the guitar playing of Slash, Edward Van Halen, and Gary Moore, among others. Don't you just hate a show-off?

'Pinky's Revenge'

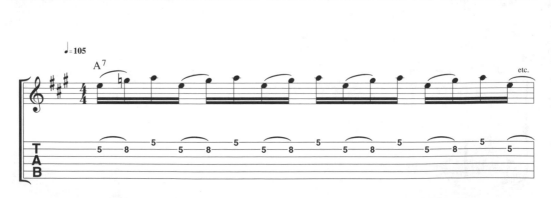

This simple hammer-on phrase is made more difficult by the fact that it's a three-note lick played in groups of four – this trick is called 'rhythmic displacement' and it's a useful way of making your playing sound more interesting than it really is!

The suggested speed of 105 b.p.m. is fine for practising the lick, but if you can get up to 120 or higher it sounds awesome!

Slash, being flash,
making cash!

'Turn On The Taps'

But surely, tapping's out-dated, gratuitous and completely passé? Sure, but we all secretly like it, don't we!

Tap with the second finger of the picking hand, and play the hammer-ons and pull-offs with the fretting hand.

'Folk Fever'

Strictly speaking, this is a folky acoustic guitar phrase, but the combination of fast pull-offs and upstrokes with the plectrum makes for a great electric lead lick.

'Rolling Fingers'

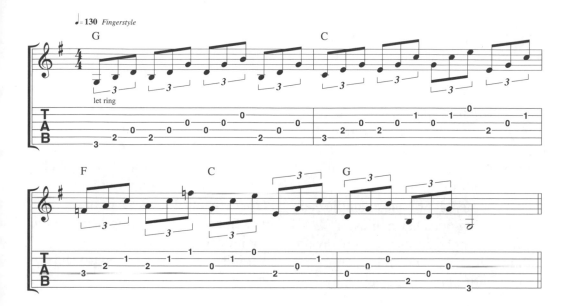

The technique shown here is called a 'banjo roll'. The thumb picks the first note in each group of three, and the first and second fingers pick the other two in a 'rolling' motion. If you can play these evenly, you can create the illusion that you can play three times fast than you actually can. Flash, tasteless and totally unnecessary!

THE TECHNIQUES THAT TASTE FORGOT

Or – "Where can I buy a can of lighter fuel at this time of night?"

'Playing behind the head'

This technique, stolen by Hendrix from bluesman T-Bone Walker, looks great on stage, but is actually dead easy to do – you don't have to play 'backwards' at all. When the guitar's on your shoulders, you'll find your fingers are actually in a really comfortable playing position, as long as you don't mind that you can't see what you're doing.

'Playing with your teeth'

Of course, our Jimi did nothing of the sort. Playing with your teeth *hurts*, for goodness sake. Just hold the guitar up to your face, gripping the body so your face is obscured, then play hammer-ons and pull-offs with the fretting hand only. It's

that easy. Velvet loon pants are, of course, optional.

'Windmilling'

Invented by Pete Townshend in the mid-60s. AKA revolving your outstretched arm at 90mph to make the audience think you're hitting a chord *really* hard. If you actually do this at speed you'll catch your thumbs on the cutaway and have to wear Elastoplast for the rest of the tour – not particularly rock 'n' roll. The 'windmill' should be as fast as possible on the (very visual) upstroke, then slow down just before you strum the chord (quite lightly) in an *upward* motion. During The Who's 1985 *Live Aid* set, Pete attempted a complex windmill/scissor-kick combination... and fell over.

Weird And Wonderful Techniques

Some riffs depend on specialist techniques for their sound. Most guitarists can manage hammer-ons, pull-offs, slides and bends, but there are other useful ideas you can employ when making up riffs. Apart from extending the musical range of the guitar, these techniques have the advantage of being fairly visual too (see previous page).

This chapter shows one example each of licks using open harmonics, violining, tapped harmonics, downward sliding gliss notes and sliding chords.

Open harmonics are achieved by gently touching the string with the fretting hand directly over the fret shown, then removing the finger immediately after you pick the note so the harmonic rings on clearly.

Tapped harmonics use a similar idea, but you tap hard onto the fret with the picking hand while fretting the note. To achieve 'violining' you should pluck the string with the guitar volume at zero, then swell the note in using the little finger of the picking hand on the volume control. The final two examples are simple fretboard slides, but used in an unusual way.

'Tuneful Harmonics'

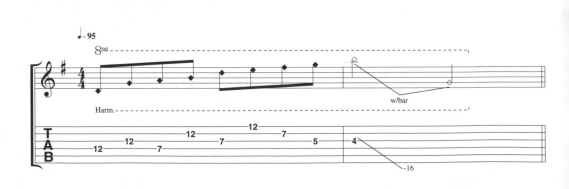

If you know where to find open harmonics (the strongest ones are over the 12th, 7th and 5th frets) you can create whole melodies with them. This example is equally effective in the key of G or E minor.

The last note features a 'dive' – play the difficult 4th fret harmonic, then depress the whammy bar all the way. The more overdrive the better!

'Fender Strad'

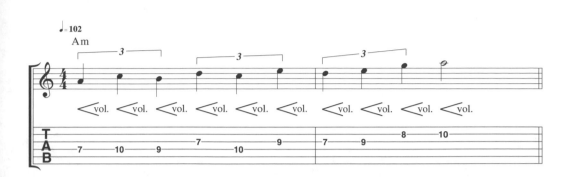

Because violining is fairly difficult to execute cleanly, it can help if you slow down the pace of the notes to give you time to work the volume control. This lick could appear in the middle of a fairly frantic A minor rock solo, creating a contrast when you go into these slower quarter note triplets.

'Tap On The Back'

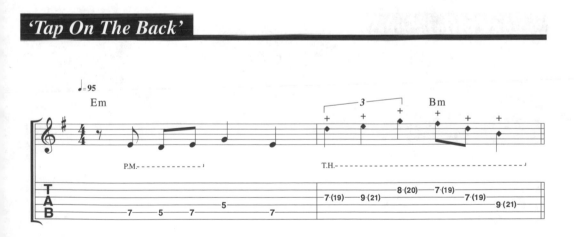

This example uses two very different techniques to give the two phrases contrasting 'voices'. After the punchy, palm-muted opening, the tapped harmonics create a bell-like, chiming effect. Fret the harmonic notes at the position shown, then tap briefly over the fret number shown in brackets. Again, distortion or overdrive will help you here.

'2-Way Slide'

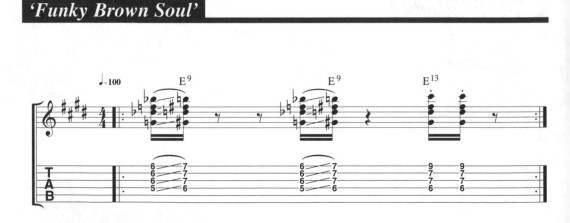

Many of us are in the habit of quickly sliding up to a note, as shown in the first bar. But sliding *down* into a note is less well-used, and it creates an unearthly, almost voice-like effect.

Although it's been used by blues players such as Peter Green and Kenny Wayne Shepherd, it was taken to its extreme by Steve Vai, who can do accurate grace-note slides over 12 frets!

'Funky Brown Soul'

And while we're at it, why shouldn't we slide into chords too? This one-bar sliding E9 lick appears all over James Brown's early recordings; its sharp down-and-up rhythms contrast with the rests in the bar – funksters call this 'hot space'. Use a clean tone, with very little reverb.

Frank Zappa admires another one of Steve Vai's long fretboard slides.

Keef – possibly the riffiest guitarist in the world?

There's an old guitar players' joke that goes something like this; "I'm a better guitarist than Jimmy Page, y'know. He didn't write *Stairway To Heaven* until he was 21, and I could play it when I was 16!"

It's all very well to be able to play other people's riffs, but if it's rock megastardom you're after, you need to be writing your own. And it's not as easy as it might seem. A good riff may only have four or five notes in it, but there are an infinite number of ways they can be used.

Still, take heart – the guitar riff as we know it has only been around for 40 years or so, so perhaps the Best Riff Of All Time has yet to be written? And perhaps you're the one to write it? Just remember me in your will, won't you!

Making Up Riffs

- Keep it short! Any riff longer than four bars without a repeat is going to lose the listener. Sometimes it doesn't even need to be as long as a whole bar.

- Steal from the best. If you can take a well-known riff and change it so that it's unrecognisable, while still sounding as good as the original, it's still 'your' riff.

- Use techniques. Slide into riffs, or parts of riffs. Use hammer-ons, pull-offs, palm mutes, bends, tapping, harmonics… whatever gives you the sound you want.

- Avoid techniques! Some of the best riffs ever recorded are just notes or chords – think of The Stones' *Satisfaction*, The Manics' *Design For Life*, or The Beatles' *Day Tripper*.

- Keep it simple. If your riff starts getting too flash, could be you're actually making up a lead lick rather than a riff. In which case you should be reading the box on the right.

- Play around the song. If you've already written some chords and a melody, put a rough version down on tape so you can hear how your riff works in context.

- Use effects. Tremolo, vibrato, chorus, and delay can all enhance riffs; and rock players shouldn't leave the house without their distortion pedals!

- Send me some riffs! joe.bennett@ndirect.co.uk

Making Up Licks

- Keep it short! The whole point of soloing using licks is that you throw them in at opportune moments. If your licks are really long, you might as well learn a whole solo by heart.

- Steal from everyone! If you see another guitarist play a great lick at a gig, ask them how they did it. Most players will be more than happy to share their knowledge with you.

- Use techniques. Licks are rarely identified purely by the notes they contain – there's usually a degree of specialist technique in there somewhere.

- Avoid getting too 'riffsome'. If you find your lick's really too repetitive, try some variations within it – or perhaps you can use it over and over as a riff!

- Don't feel you have to keep it simple. If you want to throw in you lick for effect at just the right moment, why shouldn't it be outrageously flamboyant?

- Play around different keys. If your lick works really well in the key of A, try figuring out how to play it in C, or F#. That way, you'll be able to use it in a variety of contexts.

- Avoid effects. A good lead lick might sound just as good on a battered acoustic as on a custom electric through a rack full of multi-FX

- Email me your licks! joe.bennett@ndirect.co.uk

IT'S EASY TO BLUFF

Be an instant expert with this great new series from Music Sales. Each book includes player/band biographies, a history of the guitar style, musical examples, and lots of handy tips and tricks to help you 'bluff your way through' any situation!

Blues Guitar
AM955196

Rock Guitar
AM955218

Music Theory
AM958585

Jazz Guitar
AM955185

Metal Guitar
AM955207

REALLY EASY GUITAR!

Now you can join your favourite band!
It couldn't be easier to strum and sing your favourite rock and pop classics. Each book includes easy chord boxes, simple guitar TAB and full lyrics. The high quality backing tracks on the enclosed CD give you authentic soundalike arrangements-just like the original recordings!

90s Hits
AM957715

The Beatles
NO90692

Rock Classics
AM957693

Eric Clapton
AM968462

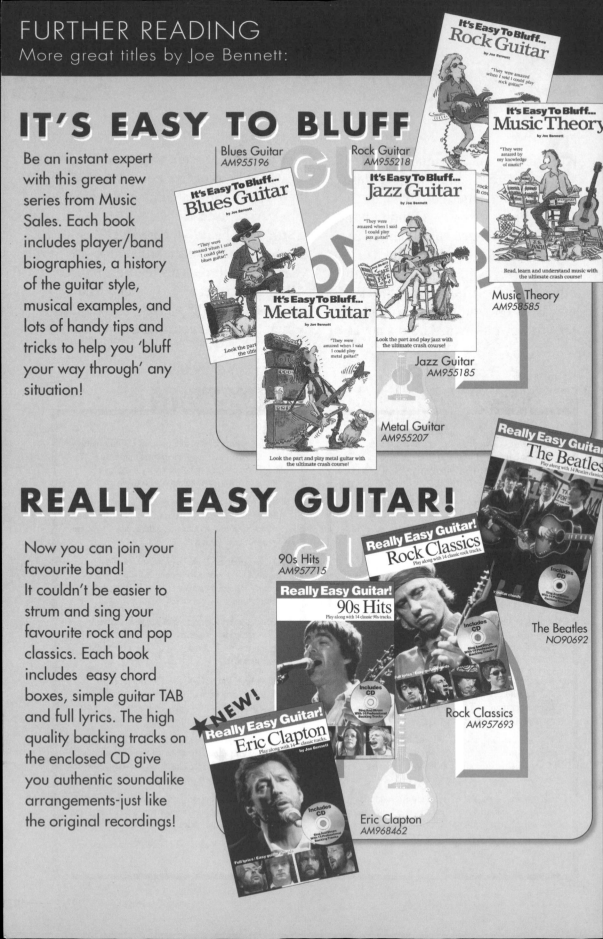